BUILDING
Online
RELATIONSHIPS

One Reader At A Time

LaShaunda C. Hoffman

HOFFMAN
CONTENT, LLC

HERE'S WHAT PEOPLE ARE SAYING ABOUT
Building Online Relationships: One Reader At A Time

"LaShaunda's book on promoting is a very detailed guide to getting your promotions on track. With years of experience, LaShaunda is sharing everything she's done and giving you the inside track on how to stay on track for a whole year. You can't go wrong with this informative manual, and it's recommended for newbies as well as seasoned authors."

–Barbara Joe Williams, author of *Forgive Us This Day*
Amazon author's page: http://goo.gl/hCOkBb
Facebook: www.facebook.com/Barbarajoe22
Twitter: www.twitter.com/BarbaraJoe22
Website: www.barbarajoe.webs.com

"LaShaunda C. Hoffman is one of our literary legends! Her work with SORMAG has launched many authors on to greatest. If there is anyone capable of providing authors with a roadmap to success it's LaShaunda. She has spent years cultivating relationships and marketing strategies that are needed to market and promote books. Her book, *Building Online Relationships – One Reader At A Time*, is a written legacy of those master years and a way for upcoming artists and authors to reach their full potential. If I were a betting woman, I would bet the house on LaShaunda C. Hoffman and all of her new adventures."

–Ella Curry, President of **EDC** Creations
Black Pearls Magazine Online-Founder
Black Authors Network Radio-Founder
Social Media Expert - Internet Publicist - Brand Strategist

"Stepping out and revealing your book to the masses can be overwhelming and scary. LaShaunda Hoffman has been able to take that fear and turn it into action. The how is answered and the steps are given. I only wished that I had this resource when I first came out."

—Tamika Newhouse

"I'm a fan of SORMAG, have been since LaShaunda Hoffman started her multicultural magazine in 2000. When I became a published author, SORMAG was first and still remains one of my main online book promotion sources. LaShaunda offers twenty-five, easy-to-digest lessons that not only will guide a newbie author, but the veteran author who has grown weary of doing the same old promotions with no results. I can guarantee she will start the book marketing juices flowing for many authors with her debut, *Building Online Relationships One Reader At a Time.* "

—Tyora Moody, Author of the Serena Manchester Series, Victory Gospel Series and the Eugeena Patterson Mysteries.

"There can never be too many books on marketing and promoting and this one should definitely be added to your arsenal when it comes to promoting your books. LaShaunda has done an excellent job on doing all the work for you, except the implementation. She has broken each chapter down by lessons (twenty-five to be exact) and each lesson has its own topic. She has covered most, if not all, of the topics that any author will be faced with when trying to promote their work. In the back of the book she has included worksheets to keep you more organized and efficient. This tool will help any author use their time more wisely. Without a doubt, *Building Online Relationships: One Reader At A Time* is well worth the investment. Her years as a business professional have qualified her to be an expert in her field."

–Paulette Harper, author and owner of WNL Virtual Tours

"I believe that when it comes to online promotion, LaShaunda Hoffman and SORMAG are one of the best in the industry! When I started out in the literary industry several years ago, LaShaunda was one of the people I wanted to emulate. She was featuring some of my favorite authors and I was so very impressed. I've studied and followed

LaShaunda and will continue to do so in hopes that I can one day be as proficient as she is."

–Renee Spivey, Literary Signature Services

"All of her years of experience are DETAILED in one solid format. A clear and concise action guide for any author who is serious about promoting their book."

–Debra Owsley of Simply Said Reading Accessories

www.simply-said.net

www.simplysaidreadingaccessories.blogspot.com

odebdeb@aol.com

"5 out of 5 stars! *Building Online Relationships: One Reader At A Time* is the most comprehensive guide for online promotions on the market today. Hoffman gives writers step-by-step tips on how to successfully promote their books online while continuing to focus on the primary goal of writing. There is a wealth of information, including how to successfully do a blog tour, how to create an online promotional budget, and figuring out who your reader is. Hoffman also includes schedules and worksheets to help the writer to achieve specific goals on a daily, weekly, monthly, and yearly basis. This book is not something to be read in one sitting. The book is meant to be read in stages so that you can complete the worksheets and calendars according to the different goals you're trying to reach. One of the many standout tips of this book is to not become a "drive by" author in different social media groups and forums. Many writers need to definitely take heed of this advice. *Building Online Relationships: One Reader At A Time* provides excellent information not just for writers, but other literary professionals can benefit from some of these tips as well."

–Radiah Hubbert of Urban Reviews

Published by
Hoffman Content, LLC
8816 Manchester Rd, #231
Brentwood, MO 63144

ISBN: 978-0-9961245-0-8

Library of Congress Control Number: 2015911719

Cover and Interior Design by TWASolutions.com

To receive free email newsletters delivering tips and updates about promotions, register directly at http://lashaundahoffman.com

DEDICATION

This workbook is dedicated to newly published authors and writers with a few books under their belts who feel overwhelmed when it comes to online promotion. Hopefully, these lessons will teach you how to create a plan that will assist you in introducing you and your book to the reading public.

IN MEMORY OF

Brenda Joann Turner
(1947-2011)

My mother, best friend and number one fan.
Thanks for believing in me.
Until we meet again.

ACKNOWLEDGEMENTS

Thank you Renee Daniel Flagler, Pat Simmons and Sylvia Hubbard, who told me at the Fall Into Literature Conference in 2011 to write something to help writers learn how to promote. Advice taken.

To all the authors I love and promoted and the loyal readers of SORMAG, without you there would be no SORMAG. Thank you.

To my promotion sisters: Martina Tee Royals, Ella Curry, Radiah Hubbert, Debra Owsley, Renee Spivey, TaNisha Webb, Orsayor Simmons, Lasheera Lee, Sharon Lucas and brother Wayne Jordan. You share my love of promotion. Thank you for your friendship.

To The Hotties: Michele Robinson, Shaun Williams, Sean Taylor Young, Michelle Wilkes, Brenda Woodbury, Angel Cason, Lisa White, Melissa Scriven, Jeanette Cogdell, Betty Williams Phyllis Redus, Carolyn Hector Hall, Trinette Blackwell, Gwen Osborne, Shirion, Simmons. You started this journey with me when SORMAG was an idea. I'm grateful for our friendships.

My Literary sisters: Patricia Woodside, Kaia Alderson-Tyson, Makasha Dorsey and Ann Clay. Thank you for your friendship.

To lifelong friends: Petra Baker, Lenora Tyler, Ruth Langlois, Phyllis Haynes Emery, Christina Tillman and Adrian Logan. Thank you for believing in my dream.

Jennifer Halla-Sindelar, the best St. Louis Public Librarian ever, thank you for helping me see this title was the best for this book.

Thank you to my St. Louis Christian Writers Group: Phyllis, Ellen, Suzanne and Terri for encouraging me each month. I'm thankful for our friendship.

Thank you Paulette Nunlee for your assistance with completing the book, and our new friendship.

To my family on my mother's side, my father's side and my husband side—I love you guys.

Thank you Dr. Linda Beed, my writing mentor, whose weekly calls help keep my writing dreams on course.

Thank you LaTara V. Bussey, my business/life coach, for showing me that fear will always be there, but it doesn't have to control me.

Thank you Bridgette, Stephanie, Antoinette and Socrotiff for always believing your sister was a writer and one day there would be a book with her name on it.

Thank you Pamela Vega, Brenda Dirks, Michele Williams-Perry and Kate Swat, my sisters at work, for believing in my dream and for your encouragements over the years.

To my Virtual Tea Members: Danyelle Scroggins, Sheryl Lister, Tracee Garner, W. Parks Brigham, Dr. Linda Beed, Jeanette Hill, Maurice Gray, Cynthianna Matthews, Sharisa Robertston and Ashley Sauls. Thank you for taking me to my next level—coaching. As a teacher, I could not have asked for better students.

To my Indie sisters: Barbara Joe Williams, A'ndrea Wilson, Kianna Alexander, Angelia Vernon Menchan, Iris Bolling, Rose Jackon Beaver, Shelia Goss, Marissa Monteilh, Tyora Moody and Michelle Stimpson, thank you for paving the way and sharing your knowldge with me. I truly appreciate sitting at your feet and learning about the business.

Thank you Jessica Tilles for helping me bring this book to life. Your encouraging emails made this a wonderful experience. Thank you ladies and gentlemen for being the stars in my life and helping my writing path shine brightly. A special thank you to my family: Clyde, Nichaela, Clyde, Jr. and Sean. Prayers could not have given me a better family. I'm truly thankful you put up with my writer madness and understand why my face is glued to a laptop most days. Indeed, some days it drives you all crazy, but you've never stopped supporting my dreams and telling me that one day those dreams would become real. I love you with all my heart.

Last, but not least, I must thank God for seeing the writer inside me before I did. For whispering in my ear "You're still in control" on those days I was allowing fear to control me. I'm so blessed to have a Father like You in my life. Thank you, God, for carrying me on those days I couldn't carry myself. I look forward to the books we will write together because I know I can't do this career without You and I don't want to.

If I left anyone out, please don't take it personal. There's just not enough paper to say "thank you" to everyone, so I say it here: Thank you so much from the bottom of my heart.

CONTENTS

INTRODUCTION

You are probably wondering who I am and what I know about promotions. As founder and editor in chief of *Shades of Romance Magazine*, affectionately known as SORMAG, an online magazine promoting authors and books to a massive community of readers, I know promotions. This book was written for one reason: to share lessons learned on my journey of promoting SORMAG since 2000 so that you, too, can be successful with your promotions.

A few months after launching SORMAG, it welcomed eighteen thousand visitors, and was awarded *Writer's Digest's* "101 Best Writing Sites," which is a big deal for a new site. SORMAG has been featured in *Essence* magazine, and in 2014, it was nominated for an African American Literary Awards Show award.

For the last two years, I received the Black Pearls Literary Excellence award from Black Pearls Magazine so all that promoting was paying off.

For fifteen years, I have facilitated workshops, written articles, and monthly columns on what I know best—promotions. My online radio show and two podcasts—The Writer's Café and See Ya On The 'Net—Online Promotion Tips—are heard by thousands.

Aside from being a featured author in the *How I Met My Sweetheart* and *When Women Become Business Owners* anthologies, and currently writing a middle school fantasy, I am an ex-Navy girl working for the government who is happily married with children.

Over the years, I've learned the importance of promotion, a mailing list and online networking. These three things have helped me turn SORMAG into an award-winning, online magazine. Online promotion works because of the power of word of mouth. People will talk about you and your book, and these lessons will help you to get people talking about you and your book.

Now that you know who I am, let's talk promotion!

WHAT IS PROMOTION?

For writers, promoting and writing go hand-in-hand. If you think differently, getting your book before readers will be very hard. If no one knows your book exists, you can't make a sale.

This workbook is a guide to helping you make the best of your promotion time. To do that, we must start with one simple question: *What Is Promotion?*

Promotion is raising customer awareness of a product or brand, generating sales and creating brand loyalty.

However, I define promotion as introducing a reader to your book, selling the book to the reader and adding that reader to your community as a loyal customer.

I've heard a lot from writers who are disappointed with their promotion, be it free or paid. They believe that if they don't make a sale their promotion has failed.

This isn't true. Promotion isn't about the sale. Promotion is about keeping yourself in front of the reader so they know who you are.

People buy from people they trust. If they don't know you, they have a hard time spending their money on you.

That's why businesses advertise, so you know who they are and feel comfortable enough to patronize them. The same goes for book promotion.

You do the blog tour, you buy ads in online magazines, you do the radio interviews and you do the blog interviews, so you can introduce yourself to readers or listeners who visit these sites, magazines or shows.

Now I want you to be the book buyer.

Do you buy the book the first time you see a promotion for it?

Do you click on the link and check out the author?

Do you look it up online in the bookstores for more info?

Do you ask a friend about it?

Do you read the reviews?

The next time you see a promotion for the same book—do you buy or click delete?

Sometimes it takes a few times to decide if you want to spend your money on a book. Sometimes it takes an instant. The blurb grabs you and you CLICK.

We all want our promotion to be in front of those readers.

This workbook will assist you to create your promotions strategy. No promises are made that it will make you a bestselling author, but it will help to get your name and book in front of readers.

Do I have all the answers? No, but I can help you create a strategy that will help you get in front of readers.

Like many of you reading this, I didn't know anything about promotions when I started SORMAG, but by the time I published the first issue, I had become a pro at the game of online promotions. However, I will be the first to admit that I seek to learn something new every day. What I've learned I'm now sharing with you.

Hopefully, your questions about online promotion will be answered, and you will be steered in the right direction to creating your own plan of action.

HOW TO USE THIS WORKBOOK

After you've read this workbook, tackle one chapter at a time. Unfortunately, I can't possibly list every resource that's available to an author, so in addition to following the steps listed here, I suggest expanding your plan to include several Internet search engines.

Before you're done with this book, your favorite search engine will be your best friend. Things change daily with the Internet. After you have created list after list, you will find they no longer exist when you need them. So, it is important that you learn how to locate resources and create lists that work for you.

There are three ways to use this workbook:

1. Do each lesson and set up a plan using each lesson.
2. Skip the lessons you know and focus on the lessons you need help in.
3. Choose the lessons you are comfortable with and create a plan.

Each lesson will include:

- *LaShaunda's Tip*
- *What you can do with the lesson yearly, monthly, weekly or daily*
- *What to schedule on your calendar*
- *How to get started*
- *How you can use the lesson in your promotion*

You should start with a fresh list, with new contacts, which is why I have you conducting your own research. You will always want to have current contact information when you want to introduce yourself to sites, magazines, etc. It's hard to get past the gatekeeper when they are receiving hundreds of emails on a daily basis, so knowing who you need to contact is very important. DO YOUR RESEARCH. You will be happy you did.

Before we begin, I want to thank you for purchasing this book. My goal is to help you get in front of as many readers as you can. You can write in this workbook. However, if you're reading the ebook version, I've created worksheets you can print out. The worksheets are meant for you to use every time you create a plan for your books.

Please feel free to contact me at lashaundabooks@gmail.com for worksheets, or if you have any questions.

Calendar 1

Your calendar is an important part of your promotion. It helps keep you organized, and it's great to be able to see where you are or where you are going with your promotion.

Some writers prefer a desktop calendar or pocket calendars. Google's online calendar is also useful, and it synchronizes to your phone or tablets.

Don't move forward with this workbook until you have a calendar you can work with. Get one you feel comfortable using because if it's not what you like, you will not use it and I need you to use your calendar.

I use a pocket calendar I can place in my purse. I purchased it from Dollar Tree, who sells yearly calendars and I love the big spaces it has to write in. I carry it with me all the time, so I will know what's on the agenda daily. It has saved me many times when I had forgotten an appointment or deadline.

The best part about a calendar is I can see what I need to do and what I've accomplished. Some days it seems like I haven't done anything productive, but my calendar will prove me wrong.

You want access to your calendar daily. If you keep to

a schedule, you will find promoting to be simple instead of overwhelming. What is the release date for your book? Schedule it on your calendar. This will help in setting the time frame for your promotions. Don't have a release date? That's even better! You have time to work on your schedules.

I recommend at least *ten* promotions:

- *Three* promotions a month before the release date. You want to get readers ready for the book and stimulate possible pre-order sales.
- *Four* promotions the week your book releases.
- *Three* promotions after the release. You want to catch those readers who might have missed the previous promotions.

You can decide if you want to do more promotions, and how to break them up between free and paid. Your budget will determine this.

Ten promotions and you've started your promotion plan. That wasn't so hard. Now you're ready to figure out what promotions you want to do.

MY EXPERIENCE

Admittedly, I'm not the best when it comes to being organized. Having a calendar helps me become an organized person. I couldn't do SORMAG without one. A calendar keeps me on focus with what I'm doing daily, weekly or monthly. Once I learned more about promotion and getting organized, I started using my calendar more. I set up my yearly promotion plan, and I am able to focus on what I need to do. I can also see what I've completed for the year and what I wanted to move over to the upcoming year or drop off my plan.

It helps me with interviews and articles I feature in SORMAG. When it comes to a magazine, the last thing I want to do is use repeated content. I always want to have new content. Knowing who I've interviewed or articles I featured help me keep SORMAG with new content.

You don't have to be an organized person to use a calendar. However, you will find yourself becoming better at being organized.

CTION PLAN

LaShaunda's Tip
Use colored ink pens to keep organized: blue for writing schedule, black for promotion, red for deadlines. You can glance at your calendar and know by the colors what's on your agenda for the day.

Getting Started
Determine which calendar works for you: a pocket calendar, wall calendar or online calendar. Pick a twelve-month calendar. You want to be able to look at all the dates for the year.

Schedule Your Calendar
- What is your release date?
- Schedule ten promotion dates.
- Schedule your next lesson: Online Promotion Plan Questions.

Online Promotion
Plan Questions

To know what you don't know there are pertinent questions to be asked and answered. Bear in mind that those questions cannot be answered without a clear understanding of industry terms. This lesson has been divided into two segments to help you get started:

1. The **Glossary of Terms** is provided to help you understand questions and passages that will appear in this workbook.

2. **Answer the Questions** will help you identify what you already have and what you need to obtain.

GLOSSARY OF TERMS

Advertisement prices—Prices for advertisement on blogs, sites, magazines, radio shows, etc.

ARC—Advance Reading Copy, an uncorrected proof, or bound galley proof of a manuscript that is sent out to book reviewers.

Articles—A piece of writing about a particular subject that is included in a magazine, newspaper, etc.

Author profile—A profile for social media sites that includes a bio, website link, contact information, etc.

Author pages—A professional page for authors (i.e., Facebook, Twitter, Amazon, etc.).

Blog—A regularly updated website or web page that is written in an informal or conversational style, usually about personal opinions, activities, and experiences.

Blog tour—A virtual tour for your book or product. It is the same concept as going to a brick and mortar to hold a book signing, except it is held online on various blogs.

Book discussions—Meetings with book clubs and readers about books.

Budget—An amount of money available for spending that is based on a plan for how it will be spent.

Calendar—A list or schedule of events or activities that occur at different times throughout the year.

Chats—To talk over the Internet by sending messages back and forth in a chat room.

Database—A collection of pieces of information that is organized and used on a computer.

Email signature—The signature used for closing an email.

Forums—An online place for discussing a subject.

Genre—A category of literary works (romance, mystery, historical, suspense, etc.).

Goals—Something that you are trying to do or achieve.

Groups—An online place where people are connected by some shared activity, interest, or quality.

Guidelines—A rule or instruction that shows or tells how something should be submitted.

Introduction letter—A letter to introduce you and your book to a site, blog, magazine or radio show.

Newsletter—A short, written report that tells about the recent activities and is sent to newsletter subscribers.

Online book clubs—A group of people who meet online to talk about the books.

Online book stores—A place online that sells books.

Online events—Events (literary, workshops, seminars) that are hosted online.

Online magazines—A magazine online that contains stories, essays, pictures, etc., and is usually published every week or month.

Online radio—Radio shows hosted online, live or taped.

Platform—A declaration of the principles on which a person stands for.

Podcasts—A program (music or talk) made available in digital format for automatic download over the Internet.

Promotion—Something (such as advertising) that is done to make people aware of something and increase its sales or popularity.

Reviews—A report that gives someone's opinion about the quality of a book.

ROI—Return On Investment.

Short stories—A short, written story usually dealing with few characters: a short work of fiction.

Skype—An online website for face-to-face chats.

Social media—Forms of electronic communication (such as websites for social networking and microblogging) through which users create online communities to share information, ideas, personal messages, and other content (such as videos).

Theme—The main subject that is being discussed or described in a piece of writing.

Videos—A recording similar to a videotape but stored in digital form.

Website—A place on the World Wide Web that contains information about a person, organization, etc., and that usually consists of many web pages joined by hyperlinks.

Let's get started! I suggest you get out a pen or pencil and a pad so you can write down your answers or print out your worksheets if you are reading the ebook.

The more yeses you have the closer you are to creating your plan. If you have a lot of nos you might want to tackle those first in the lessons. Remember, you don't have to do this in one sitting. I honestly don't think you can because of all the research you will have to do. Take your time to answer these questions and you will be on your way to creating your online promotional plan.

ANSWER THE QUESTIONS

1. Why did you write this book?_____
   _____
   _____

2. What is your long-term goal for your book? _____
   _____
   _____

3. What is your short-term goal for your book?_____
   _____
   _____

4. Have you created a budget for your online promotion?

5. Do you know the best online outlets for promoting your book?

6. Do you know who your readers are?

7. Do you know where to find your readers?

8. Do you have a dedicated email for your potential readers to reach you?

9. Is your book information included in your email signature?

10. Do you have a website?

11. Do you have a database?

12. Do you have a monthly newsletter?

13. Do you own a site or blog?

14. Are you on social media?

15. Do you have author pages?

16. Do you belong to any groups/forums?

17. Do you have your own groups?

18. Have you researched the sites/blogs that promote your genre?

19. Have you made a list of sites/blogs where you can introduce yourself?

20. Have you researched their advertisement prices?

21. Have you written your introduction newsletter?

22. Have you sent out your letters to the sites/blogs?

23. Have you decided if you would do a blog tour? If yes, have you set up the blog tour?

24. Have you created at least six articles that focus on your book's theme?

25. Have you submitted the articles you created?

26. Have you researched places to submit your articles?

27. Have you researched forums/groups/lists that promote your genre?

28. Have you created your list of forums you want to be on?

29. Have you sent out letters to the forums?

30. Have you scheduled chats?

31. Have you researched online book clubs?

32. Have you researched their advertisement prices?

33. Do you know their guidelines?

34. Have you created a list of online book clubs that promote your genre?

35. Have you sent out letters of introduction?

36. Have you scheduled chats or Skype chats?

37. Have you scheduled book discussions?

38. Have you researched the online radio shows that promote your genre?

39. Have you researched their advertisement prices?

40. Do you know their guidelines?

41. Have you created your list of online radio shows you want to be on?

42. Have you sent out your letters to the online radio shows?

43. Do you have your own online radio show?

44. Have you researched online magazines that promote your genre?

45. Have you created a list of online magazines you want to be featured in?

46. Do you know their guidelines?

47. Have you requested interviews from these magazines?

48. Have you researched their advertisement prices?

49. Have you submitted articles/short stories to them?

50. Have you created podcasts?

51. Do you have themes for your podcasts?

52. How often will you create podcasts?

53. Have you researched podcasts that feature your genre?

54. Do you know what their guidelines are?

55. Have you created a list of podcasts you want to be featured on?

56. Have you created videos?

57. Do you have themes for your videos?

58. How often will you create them?

59. Have you created online events?

60. Do you have themes for your online events?

61. How often will you create them?

62. Have you researched online events that feature your genre?

63. Do you know what their guidelines are?

64. Have you created a list of online events you want to be featured in?

65. Do you have any reviews for your book?

66. Do you know which online reviewers or sites will review your genre?

67. Have you researched online reviewers?

68. Do you know what their guidelines are?

69. Have you created a list of reviewers you want to send your book to?

70. Is your book featured on online bookstores?

71. Do you know the guidelines for your book to be featured?

72. Do you have reviews on these sites?

73. Do you have an author page or profile?

74. Have you scheduled any promotions?

PROMOTION PLAN CHECKLIST
(Check areas where you need help.)

____ 1. Budget

____ 2. Email signature

____ 3. Database/email list

____ 4. Who is your reader?

____ 5. Where to find your reader?

____ 6. Articles

____ 7. Monthly newsletters

____ 8. Website/blog

____ 9. Social media

____ 10. Writer/reader sites/blogs

____ 11. Blog tours

____ 12. Submitting articles

____ 13. Forums/groups/lists

____ 14. Online book clubs

____ 15. Online radio

____ 16. Online magazines

____ 17. Online events

____ 18. Podcasts

____ 19. Videos

____ 20. Calendar

____ 21. Goals

____ 22. Creating a plan

MY EXPERIENCE

Over the years, I've compiled the above questions to help me focus on what I want to do with SORMAG promotions for the year. Knowing what I want to do with my promotion helps me move forward.

I also try to do something new each year. Maybe I'll try a new social media or maybe I'll find new blogs to visit. It helps me stay fresh and meet new people.

CTION PLAN

LaShaunda's Tip

Answering the questions honestly will assist you in setting up your calendar and creating a plan.

Remember you don't have to do everything on the checklist. Don't overwhelm yourself. Choose five to ten activities and focus on them for this year. You can always add more if you need more promotion.

Getting Started

Let's get to the fun part—making sense of all the questions you answered.

Now that you've answered these questions, you are ready to take the steps to create your online promotion plan. As I've said before, if you're clear on your "yeses" go directly to your "nos."

There are enough lessons that you can do something different each month. Don't try to do it all in one sitting. Schedule dates on your calendar and work your plan daily.

Schedule Your Calendar

Schedule a date on your calendar for the next lesson: Who Is Your Reader?

Who Is Your Reader?

Do you know who your readers are?

The best way to begin creating your promotion plan is by identifying your reader. Most writers aren't thinking about their readers when they are writing. However, that is the perfect time to imagine who will be reading your books. Knowing your reader will help you focus on content that will touch them emotionally.

TYPES OF READERS

A Loyal Reader is always reading a book and suggesting books to friends.

A Busy Reader likes to read, but only when time permits.

Every Now And Then Reader will read when they have nothing else to do.

Crowd Reader will read when the book becomes popular and they want to be a part of the crowd.

I Don't Read Reader doesn't care for reading.

Knowing what type of reader you seek will help with your plan to reach them.

The reader profile on the next page will help you figure out your ideal reader.

MY EXPERIENCE

When I started SORMAG, I thought I knew my readers as women who read romance. However, as I talked more with my readers, I realized they are women, ages 25 to 75, who read one or two books a month, are college educated, married and enjoy talking about books.

Knowing this information helps me when it comes to topics for SORMAG. You need to know who your reader is so you know what to write for them.

YOUR READER PROFILE

What age is your reader? _____

What gender? _____

Where does your reader live? _____

_____

What is your reader's annual salary? _____

What is your reader's educational level? _____

_____

What is your reader's marital status? _____

What type of life does your reader have? _____

_____

_____

What type of books does your reader read? _____

_____

_____

How often does your reader buy books? _____

_____

_____

How often does your reader read books? _____

_____

What are your reader's guilty pleasures? _____

_____

_____

What magazines, blogs or websites does your reader read? ___

_____

_____

Where can you find your reader online? _____

_____

_____

Where can you find your reader offline? _____

_____

_____

How do you plan to keep in touch with your reader?

_____

_____

_____

CTION PLAN

LaShaunda's Tip
Knowing your readers is very important when it comes to promotion. I promote romance-based books, which means from time to time I have to decline a book because of it not appealing to my readers. Of course, the response would be, "Oh, my book is for everyone." We all hope our books are for everyone, however you will drive yourself crazy trying to cater to everyone. Find your niche and focus on those readers. You will know where to find them and you won't waste your money promoting on a romance website or blog when your book is about mass murders with no romance between the pages.

Getting Started
- Fill out the reader profile.
- Are you surprised by whom you think your reader is?
- Have you met this reader?
- Is she/he part of your followers now?

Schedule Your Calendar
Pick a day and set an actual time you can sit down and learn about your reader.

Schedule time on your calendar for the next lesson: How To Attract Readers.

Promotion Plan
- **Yearly**: Revisit these questions for each book you publish.
- **Daily**: Try to meet a new reader every day.

How To Attract Readers

How do you attract readers to your work?

WHERE ARE YOUR READERS?

Knowing where your readers are will help you determine how to attract them.

- Are they subscribed to your mailing list or your newsletter?—You want readers to be a part of your community.

- Where are they online—on social media, in groups, on blogs, in book clubs?—You have to determine which platforms to sign up for by knowing which platforms readers are using. The same goes for groups, blogs or book clubs. You don't want to participate in groups, blogs or book clubs that don't feature your reader base.

- Are they reading online magazines, sites or blogs?—Knowing which magazines, sites or blogs they are reading will help you determine where you should promote.

- Are they listening to podcasts, online radio, or watching videos?—Knowing which podcasts or online radio they are listening to, or videos they are watching will help you determine where you should promote.

Now it's time to make your presence known. Invite them to your homes on the Internet. Here are a few ways to do this:

1. Email Signature—Is your online business card. Don't send out a message without it. Include the addresses of all your online places, including an option for them to opt-in to something (e.g., mailing list, newsletter, etc.) that will keep them connected to you.

2. Website/Blog—Will draw readers who are interested in learning about you and your books. Make sure to include link to your social media homes.

3. Mailing List—Allows readers to opt-in to learn more about you and your books.

4. Newsletter—Allows readers to opt-in to learn more about you and your books.

5. Articles/Blogs—Will allow you to offer content that will draw new readers.

6. Other Blogs—Commenting on other blogs will introduce you to new readers.

7. Blog Tours—Visiting other blogs introduces you to the blog readership.

8. Forums/Lists—Participating in forums or lists introduces you to new readers.

9. Online Book Clubs—Interacting with book clubs introduces you to their readers.

10. Social Media—Interacting on social media introduces you to new readers.

11. Online Radio—Participating as a guest or part of a panel introduces you to the radio listeners. Or host your own radio show and build your readership base.

12. Online Magazines—Being featured in magazines introduces you to the magazine readers.

13. Online Events—Participating in online events introduces you to the participants in the events, such as workshops, book release parties, teleseminars and conferences.

14. Podcasts—Creating podcasts or participating in podcasts you can broadcast introduces you to new readers.

15. Videos—Creating videos or participating in videos introduces you to new readers.

16. Chat Rooms—Participating in chats will introduce you to new readers.

Always remember to take the opportunity to introduce yourself and your book to new readers and invite them to join your mailing list.

This may seem like a lot of promoting, and it can be at times. However, this book will help you break it up into bite size chunks so you can have time to promote and write.

You don't have to do all the sixteen ideas I've shared. Pick a few to focus on and you will begin to meet more readers.

This list is where you can start to meet new readers. Make a monthly goal of meeting new readers and adding them to your community. The more readers you meet the more who know about your book.

MY EXPERIENCE

Each lesson in this book is my experience in reaching new readers for SORMAG. I joined forums/groups/lists. I wrote articles, I hosted blog tours, I hosted radio shows and conducted radio interviews. I participated in online book clubs and chats. I hosted online events, workshops and podcasts. I've been video interviewed. I've been in many chat rooms with tons of readers.

It was a day-by-day plan to introduce SORMAG to readers. I learned it takes time. It's not going to happen overnight.

CTION PLAN

LaShaunda's Tip
Knowing your genre/niche will help you find readers. There is a group, organization, list, magazine and radio show for every niche or genre. If you can't find one, you can create your own. I did it with SORMAG and my first online writers group. Check out Facebook, Google Plus, and LinkedIn to create your own space online.

Getting Started
Find your readers by using these ideas:
- Find five online book clubs that read your genre.
- Find five online groups that read your genre.
- Find five online blogs that read/promote your genre.
- Find five online websites that read/promote your genre.
- Find five online radio and podcasts that promote your genre.

Schedule Your Calendar
Finding readers isn't a one-day process. Develop the daily habit of searching for new readers.

In *Getting Started*, I've started you with four ideas to research. Schedule five dates to research each idea.

Schedule time on your calendar for the next lesson—Online Promotion Goals.

Promotion Plan
- **Yearly**: You will always be searching for new places to find readers. Look for two to five new places every year.

- **Daily**: Pick one of the suggestions and focus on it to meet new readers.

IDEAS YOU CAN USE TO PROMOTE YOUR BOOK

BOOK CLUBS
- Book discussions
- Q/A sessions
- Skype interviews
- Telephone chats
- Featured author for the day

GROUPS
- Present a workshop
- Expert for the day
- Host a contest
- Host a launch party
- Offer a free copy of your book in exchange for a review

BLOGS
- Write an article
- Create a mini course
- Book excerpt
- Guest blogger
- Comment on blogs

WEBSITES
- Featured author
- Answer questions for the day

- Offer to write a column
- Create a podcast
- Host a giveaway

FORUMS/LISTS
- Daily writing workshop
- Post a chapter of your new book
- Featured author—talk about theme of book
- Critique someone's chapter
- Answer craft questions

Online Promotion *Goals*

Creating Your Goals

Do you set SMART Goals?

What are SMART Goals? SMART is a term created by George T. Doran, which stands for: **S**pecific, **M**easurable, **A**ttainable, **R**ealistic, **T**imely.

Specific: Your goals should be very specific.

Measurable: Your goals should be measurable, so you know when you've reached them.

Attainable: Your goals should be attainable. Don't set goals you'll never reach.

Realistic: Your goals should be realistic, something you can complete and have control over.

Timely: Your goals should have a deadline. You want to complete your goals, not have one that is never-ending.

Your goals for the year are what we will use to complete your unique plan of action.

Most goals can't be completed in a day, so we will take each goal and break it down to a monthly goal, then a weekly goal, then a daily goal. The daily goal is what you will put on your calendar.

You will do this for each goal until you have a full calendar for the year.

Each month, you will have an agenda for what you need to do to complete your monthly goals.

You will move forward in your promotion and you will have a schedule so you don't feel overwhelmed with promoting.

A Few Questions To Get You
Started With Setting Your Goals

What events would you like to attend this year? _____

_____

_____

_____

Would you like to go on a blog tour? How many?_____

_____

_____

_____

Will you be sending out a newsletter? _____

_____

_____

_____

Will it be an email newsletter or one hosted on your website?

_____

_____

_____

How often will you send it out?_____

_____

_____

_____

What type of content will you include? _____

_____

_____

_____

What date will you send it out? _____

_____

_____

_____

Will you write a blog? _____

_____

_____

_____

How often will you write a blog? _____

_____

_____

_____

What will you write about? _____

_____

Will you write the content or find it elsewhere? _____

_____

_____

_____

What dates will your blog posts go live? _____

_____

_____

_____

Will you write articles? _____

_____

_____

_____

What will you write about? _____

_____

_____

_____

Will you have a theme? _____

_____

_____

_____

Will you submit the articles to article submissions sites? _____

_____

_____

_____

Will you include articles on your site?_____

_____

Will you submit to online sites/magazines? _____

_____

_____

_____

When will the articles be posted? _____

_____

_____

_____

Will you host chats? _____

_____

_____

_____

How often? _____

_____

_____

_____

What dates? _____

_____

_____

_____

Will you host workshops/courses? _____

_____

_____

How often? _____

_____

_____

What dates? _____

_____

_____

Will you have contests? _____

_____

_____

How often? _____

_____

What dates? _____

_____

_____

Will you send out review copies? _____

_____

_____

How often? _____

_____

What dates? _____

_____

_____

Where to? _____

_____

_____

Will you set up meetings with book clubs? _____

_____

_____

_____

How often? _____

What dates? _____

_____

_____

Which book clubs? _____

_____

_____

What social media will you use? _____

_____

_____

Which social media is fun for you? _____

_____

_____

_____

How often would you like to be on social media? _____

_____

_____

Will you use tools to maintain a presence on social media? ___

_____

_____

_____

Will you join social media groups? Which ones? _____

_____

_____

_____

Will you create a group for you and/or your book? _____

_____

_____

_____

Will you create a group based on a topic/theme? _____

_____

_____

_____

Will you create social media content? _____

_____

_____

What type of content will you create? _____

_____

_____

_____

What tools will you use to create your content? _____

_____

_____

_____

Will you use videos? _____

_____

_____

Do you enjoy being in front of the camera? _____

_____

_____

_____

What type of content will you create? _____

_____

_____

_____

What tools will you use to create your content? _____

_____

_____

_____

Will you create podcasts? _____

_____

_____

What type of content will you create? _____

_____

_____

_____

What tools will you use to create your content? _____

_____

_____

_____

Would you like to be featured on other podcasts? _____

_____

_____

Do you know who has podcast shows? _____

_____

_____

_____

Have you scheduled any online chats? _____

_____

_____

_____

Who would you like to chat with? _____

_____

_____

_____

Do you know how to use chatting software? _____

_____

_____

Will you do online radio shows? _____

_____

_____

_____

Will you create your own online radio show? _____

_____

_____

_____

Whose show would you like to be a guest on? _____

_____

_____

Will you promote on online magazines? _____

_____

_____

_____

Which magazines would you like to be featured on? _____

_____

_____

_____

What dates are you featured? _____

_____

_____

_____

Will you pay for promotion? _____

_____

Which promotions did you purchase and what dates? _____

_____

_____

_____

Do you have any free promotion plans? _____

_____

_____

_____

Where/dates? _____

_____

_____

Will you create your own promotions? _____

_____

_____

_____

Do you have any promotion plans for the holidays? _____

_____

_____

_____

What are the dates? _____

_____

_____

Will you create marketing material? _____

_____

_____

_____

What will you create? _____

_____

_____

_____

Do you have a mailing list? _____

_____

_____

_____

How often do you maintain it? _____

_____

_____

Do you have plans to grow it? _____

_____

_____

_____

What are your plans? _____

_____

_____

_____

MY EXPERIENCE

When I first started SORMAG, I didn't write down goals. I just published issues. As I learned more about running a magazine and a business, I learned how important goals were for moving forward.

Each year I write out yearly goals. Sometimes I complete them and sometimes I don't, but I'm satisfied with what I do complete because it means I'm moving forward. I'm helping SORMAG grow.

PROMOTION GOALS FOR THE YEAR
(Example)

1. Blog Tour

2. Radio Interviews—one a month

3. Magazine Interviews—one a month

4. Create Podcasts—one a month

5. Write Articles—one a month

6. Blog—twice a week

7. Newsletter—monthly

8. Videos—book trailer

9. Videos—writing course

10. Guest Blogger—one every other month

PROMOTION GOALS FOR THE YEAR

1. _____

2. _____

3. _____

4. _____

5. _____

6. _____

7. _____

8. _____

9. _____

10. _____

11. _____

12. _____

13. _____

14. _____

15. _____

16. _____

PROMOTION GOALS FOR THE MONTH
(Example)

JANUARY
Research Online Radio Shows
Create Podcasts
Write Articles
Blog
Newsletter

FEBRUARY
Write Introduction Letters for Radio Interviews
Create Podcasts
Write Articles
Blog
Newsletter
Guest Blogger

MARCH
Research Online Magazine
Create Podcasts
Write Articles
Blog
Newsletter

APRIL
Write Introduction Letter For Magazines
Create Podcasts
Write Articles
Blog
Newsletter
Guest Blogger

MAY
Write Introduction Letters for Magazine Interviews
Create Podcasts
Write Articles
Blog
Newsletter

JUNE
Create Book Trailer
Create Podcasts
Write Articles
Blog
Newsletter
Guest Blogger

JULY
Create Writing Course
Create Podcasts
Write Articles
Blog
Newsletter

AUGUST
Schedule Blog Tour
Write Blog Tour Letters
Create Podcasts
Write Articles
Blog
Newsletter
Guest Blogger

SEPTEMBER
Create Podcasts
Write Articles
Blog
Newsletter

OCTOBER
Create Podcasts
Write Articles
Blog
Newsletter
Guest Blogger

NOVEMBER
Create Podcasts
Write Articles
Blog
Newsletter

DECEMBER
Create Podcasts
Newsletter
Guest Blogger

PROMOTION GOALS FOR THE MONTH

JANUARY

1. _____
2. _____
3. _____
4. _____
5. _____

FEBRUARY

1. _____
2. _____
3. _____
4. _____
5. _____

MARCH

1. _____
2. _____
3. _____
4. _____
5. _____

APRIL

1. _____
2. _____
3. _____
4. _____
5. _____

MAY

1. _____
2. _____
3. _____
4. _____
5. _____

JUNE

1. _____
2. _____
3. _____
4. _____
5. _____

JULY

1. _____
2. _____
3. _____
4. _____
5. _____

AUGUST

1. _____
2. _____
3. _____
4. _____
5. _____

SEPTEMBER

1. _____
2. _____
3. _____
4. _____
5. _____

OCTOBER

1. _____
2. _____
3. _____
4. _____
5. _____

NOVEMBER

1. _____
2. _____
3. _____
4. _____
5. _____

DECEMBER

1. _____
2. _____
3. _____
4. _____
5. _____

PROMOTION GOALS FOR THE WEEK
(Example)

1st WEEK
Blog posts
Content for newsletter

2nd WEEK
Research online radio shows
Set up newsletter

3rd WEEK
Write articles

4th WEEK
Create podcasts

5th WEEK
Load podcasts

PROMOTION GOALS FOR THE WEEK

1st WEEK

1. _____
2. _____
3. _____
4. _____
5. _____

2nd WEEK

1. _____
2. _____
3. _____
4. _____
5. _____

3rd WEEK

1. _____
2. _____
3. _____
4. _____
5. _____

4th WEEK

1. _____
2. _____
3. _____
4. _____
5. _____

5th WEEK

1. _____
2. _____
3. _____
4. _____
5. _____

PROMOTION GOALS FOR THE DAY
(Example)

MONDAY
Write two blog posts
Answer questions on blog
Visit forums

TUESDAY
Social media
Answer questions in groups
Answer emails

WEDNESDAY
Content for newsletter

THURSDAY
Blog visits

FRIDAY
Book clubs

SATURDAY
Social media
Create graphics

SUNDAY
Set up blog for the week
Schedule social media posts
Answer emails

PROMOTION GOALS FOR THE DAY

MONDAY

1. _____
2. _____
3. _____
4. _____
5. _____

TUESDAY

1. _____
2. _____
3. _____
4. _____
5. _____

WEDNESDAY

1. _____
2. _____
3. _____
4. _____
5. _____

THURSDAY

1. _____
2. _____
3. _____
4. _____
5. _____

FRIDAY

1. _____
2. _____
3. _____
4. _____
5. _____

SATURDAY

1. _____
2. _____
3. _____
4. _____
5. _____

SUNDAY

1. _____

2. _____

3. _____

4. _____

5. _____

CTION PLAN

LaShaunda's Tip

Writing down goals allowed me to see the progress I made toward my goals for SORMAG. Knowing where you want to go with your promotion is very important to your writing career. Make time to create your goals for the year.

Getting Started

1. Look at the answers you gave for your goals and turn them into goals.
2. Print out your worksheets or write in your workbook and start with your yearly goals.
3. Which questions can you focus on for your yearly goals?
4. Now take those goals and create monthly goals.
5. Break your monthly goals into weekly goals.
6. Finally, break the weekly goals into daily goals.
7. You will schedule these goals on your calendar.

Schedule Your Calendar

• Schedule your daily goals on your calendar.

- Schedule time on your calendar for the next lesson—Online Promotion Budget.
- Schedule a day and set an actual time you can sit down and write out your budget for your promotion.
- Schedule a day or two to research paid advertising on sites/magazines/online radio, etc.

Promotion Plan

Yearly—You want to create goals each year. Take time to revisit your goals from the previous year. Did you complete them? Do you need to reschedule for the coming year?

Monthly—Look at your goals for the month. Did you complete them? Do you need to reschedule for the next month?

Weekly—Look at your goals for the week. Did you complete them? Do you need to reschedule for the next week?

Daily—Look at your goals for the day. Did you complete them? Do you need to reschedule for the next day?

Online Promotion Budget

Have you created a budget for your online promotion?

Your strategy for your project has to have a budget. If your publisher provides an advance or as a self-published author you set aside funds for marketing, you need to decide how it will be spent.

I can hear you asking, "What money?" I'm laughing right along with you, but if you have to, you can find the money. Having a budget, even a small one, is important to promoting your books.

This workbook will give you many ideas for free promotions, but there will come a time when you will have to spend money to promote your book. Having a budget will help you not overspend and show you where your funds are going.

Example: A budget of $100 will get you a few sites to work with, which is good. But remember this is a business; you can only get freebies for so long. Eventually those sites will ignore your emails because they can no longer support you if you don't support them.

I recommend setting a monthly budget. What you can set aside will be determined by the yearly budget you create.

This budget will help with planning your promotional schedule. If you don't have a large promotional budget, you will have to make time to find more free promotions.

WHAT IS A PROMOTION BUDGET?

A promotion budget is a budget that includes what you need to promote your book and where you want to promote your book.

Below is a sample budget. It can be used as a place to start your budget. Remember each budget is different because each book and how you promote it will vary.

MY EXPERIENCE

I started SORMAG on a no-budget plan. Something I don't recommend. During that time I had to pay for web hosting, which was my monthly budget. It came out of my own pocket because I wasn't making a dime with the magazine. I hadn't learned how to monetize SORMAG.

Once I started making money with SORMAG, I created a budget to cover my financial needs and my promotional needs. Having a budget made running SORMAG so much easier because I knew what I could and couldn't afford to do with promotion.

ONLINE PROMOTION BUDGET
(Example)

Estimate Budget: $2,000.00

PROMOTIONAL NEEDS	COST ($)
Website	250.00
Web hosting	120.00
Domain name	12.00
Email marketing system	120.00
Website ads	150.00
Online magazine ads	150.00
Facebook ads	100.00
Twitter ads	100.00
Blog tours	200.00
Graphics	150.00
Review mailings	150.00
Giveaway prizes	100.00
Online radio ads	100.00
Arc copies	150.00
Budget Spent	**1,852.00**

ONLINE PROMOTION BUDGET

Estimate Budget: $_____

PROMOTIONAL NEEDS	COST ($)
Website	_____
Web hosting	_____
Domain name	_____
Email marketing system	_____
Website ads	_____
Online magazine ads	_____
Facebook ads	_____
Twitter ads	_____
Blog tours	_____
Graphics	_____
Review mailings	_____
Giveaway prizes	_____
Online radio ads	_____
Arc copies	_____
Budget Spent	_____

CTION PLAN

LaShaunda's Tip
A budget is very important to your writing business. Determine what you can set aside for the promotion of your book.

Getting Started
Budget considerations:
- Advertisement
- Website
- Business cards
- Web hosting
- Domain
- Email marketing system
- Marketing material
- Ad space
- Promotional items

What is your budget for this year? _____

Schedule Your Calendar
- Schedule time on your calendar for the next lesson—Email Address/Email Signature.
- Schedule time to research advertisement and promotion items.

Promotion Plan
YEARLY—Most of your budget will be determined by the prices you need for ad space and other promotional items. Take

some time to research prices. You want the current prices, not estimated prices.

After you have all the prices you need, add up the prices you need for your budget. Does it match what you've put aside for promotion?

Once you have your budget, you're ready to move forward.

Email Address/
Email Signature

7

Is your book information included in
your email signature?

EMAIL ADDRESS

Even though this book is about online promotion, there might
be a few of you who do not have an email address. Maybe you
don't own a computer and use the library computer to get online.
Or maybe you only use Facebook to reach your fans. I'm talking
to you right now.

You need an email address. You can't continue to promote
without it. You're missing out on communicating with others
who do have an email account. There are many free accounts out
there (Yahoo!, Hotmail, Gmail, Outlook). If you have a website,
you have an email account associated with your hosting. Put this
book down and sign up for an account or create an account with
your hosting.

I highly suggest having at least three email addresses: one for
your fans, one for your business and one for other information.

While having three email accounts may seem like more work for you, it actually cuts your time when it comes to promotion. Remember I mentioned staying organized? Three emails will help you.

I know that I've received emails from authors who missed an interview email because it got lost in their full email accounts. If they had their accounts as I suggested they wouldn't have had this problem.

Remember I mentioned making time for promotion? Wading through emails, looking for promotional opportunities, cuts into your writing time. Also, when you're on deadline you don't have time to go through emails, especially when they surpass the one hundred mark.

When you have an email that is dedicated for business only, you will click on and read through for those promotional opportunities. Hopefully it won't reach the one hundred mark and you can click on the most important emails, like those that are requesting an interview.

When you've finished with deadline hell, then you have time to read fan email. You'll be happy to see this email account that only has emails from the fans who love your writing.

The third email account can be looked at when you have time to catch up on email.

Don't make the media hunt you down. Make sure your email addresses are listed on your website, blog, social media pages and your promotional items (bookmarks, book covers, business cards, etc.).

EMAIL SIGNATURE

Your email signature is the first most important part of your book promotion plan. Why is this important? Your email is something you use on a daily basis. This is the best form of free promotion you can have. You can be creative with it and you can change it up daily, weekly or monthly. Now that you are a published writer, you never want to send out an email that doesn't include a signature.

I meet many authors because of their email signatures. They announced their new book, and that's all I need to introduce myself to them.

If you don't have an email signature, don't worry, the next step you want to take is to create a signature line for when you send out emails. You want the reader to take notice and hopefully click on the link and find out more about you.

WHAT IS A SIGNATURE?

A signature is a mini bio. I've seen some signatures that introduce the author, some that introduce a book and some that introduce a site. That's the fun part, you can come up with something creative each week or month.

Below are samples of email signatures, including mine for SORMAG:

LaShaunda C. Hoffman
Shades Of Romance Magazine Publisher
http://www.sormag.blogspot.com/

Sample writer's signature:

Shelia M. Goss
http://www.sheliagoss.com/
Delilah & Savannah's Curse—IN STORES NOW

> *"Savannah's Curse is an action-packed mystery with unexpected culprits. Shelia M. Goss brings readers a new side of her talent by entering a different genre. It is suspenseful with twists and turns that will keep readers turning pages. I recommend this book to others."* ~ Teresa Beasley, APOOO Book Club

Depending on where you send them, there are a few rules when it comes to signatures. If you're sending out an email from your email account, you're free to have as long of a signature as you like.

If you're posting or responding to a message on a list or forum, you have to make sure you know what their policy is on signatures. Some lists don't like a lot of promotion and will block your message or delete it if they think you're doing too much promotion.

I recommend keeping your signature to four lines. This gives you enough space to play with and most links and forums will permit you that many lines.

MY EXPERIENCE

An email signature has introduced me to many writers. My signature has introduced me to different opportunities. Some people don't even sign their emails, leaving you wondering who wrote it. If you don't include a signature, end your emails with your name. Not all email addresses say who is sending the email.

Always be professional when it comes to emails. I learned the hard way that using slang almost cost me a client because the client read it wrong. Keep it professional and you won't have any misunderstandings.

CTION PLAN

LaShaunda's Tip

Your email is how you communicate with your readers and people you want to help you promote your books. Create a professional email address and make sure you place it on everything that needs your contact information.

Getting Started

- Create three email accounts (fan, business, personal).
- Add a signature to your email accounts.
- Create three different signatures.

For your signature, you'll want:

Name
Title of Book
Date of release (or twenty-five words or fewer blurbs)
Website link

If you can, add a little color and hyperlink to your website link so the reader can click on it and see your book or site.

Most email systems let you add signatures to your outgoing mail. Check out the options for your email system.

If you're posting on groups, forums or lists, copy and paste your signature in your posts. Don't forget to check guidelines before you do.

Schedule Your Calendar

- Schedule a date to sit down and create your email signature.
- Schedule your updates for your email signature for the year on your calendar.
- Schedule time on your calendar for the next lesson—Website/Blog

Promotion Plan
YEARLY

- Create an email account.
- Add email to website, social media, and marketing material.

MONTHLY

- Create an email signature.
- Add your email signature to your email account (check out the option section).
- Update your signature monthly.

HOW TO USE YOUR SIGNATURE FOR PROMOTION

1. To announce new book release
2. To announce coming soon books
3. To announce contest
4. To announce blog tour
5. To announce new website or blog

Website/Blog

Do you own a site or blog?

Your website is your home base. You always want to bring the reader to your home. This is the place you keep them informed on what's happening with you and your books.

It is the second most important part of your promotion plan. If you can fit it into your budget, get your own site, with your name as the domain name. This makes it so easy for readers to type in your name.com to find you—the easier for them to remember, the easier for them to return.

The website is the best way to start your online promotion. This is a place where you can showcase your writing articles, short stories and excerpts of your books.

Many writers are using blogs as their home base because they are more interactive. I suggest you choose which one works for you and fits into your schedule. If you're not going to make time to update a blog weekly or monthly, then the website works well for you because you can update monthly or once a year, depending on how your books are released.

Your website/blog is a perfect place for introducing you and your books to potential readers. The object of your website is to keep the readers coming back. By offering different features, you're sure to bring the readers back.

Here are a few features you might want to have on your site/blog:

CONTACT ME

This is one of the most important features on the site. You won't believe how many authors don't have a contact me link. Not having a contact page is a sure way to miss a new fan or someone interested in inviting you to speak or attend an event.

You always want a link to how to get in touch with you: snail mail, email or social media.

I recommend you have a separate email just for this link. When you check it, you know it's from someone who visited your site.

Many authors are using the contact me form, which works great for readers wanting to sign up for your mailing list or newsletter. However, when it comes to media it can be a deterrent, as most won't take the time to fill out the form.

Include an email for the media to contact you. Don't miss an opportunity because there is only one way to contact you.

EMAIL MAILING LIST

The second most important feature on your site is your mailing list. This is your way of capturing the visitors to your site. Makes no sense to have a site and not invite the visitors to join your community. The whole point of promotion is to build your community. You do this by including a link or form on your site for those visitors who want to keep up with what's happening with their favorite author. This is an opt-in option. Readers sign themselves up.

BIO/ABOUT ME

An introduction of you and why you write is a must for any site. I suggest you add a picture. Readers like to see what their favorite author looks like.

ARTICLES

Articles are a good way to show readers you can write. It also can be used as a tool to teach others from your experience, and a way to draw readers back to your site.

You can offer a different article each month (bring the reader back) or feature three or four that stay on your site.

NEWSLETTER

Another way to keep your fans updated on what's happening with your writing career is through a newsletter. In the newsletter, you want to feature all the current events that are happening in your career.

You can have a link that features the newsletter on your site or a sign up form for your email newsletter. Remember you are always trying to build your fan base.

PRESS KIT

Many authors feature online press kits. It's a quick way for the media and fans to get information about you and your books. Always include a contact email on this page.

FORUMS

Forums are another great way to communicate with your readers. They can post a message and to their surprise, you can answer them. This is an excellent tool to get feedback on your books. It's also another way to bring the readers back to your site so you can interact with them.

GUESTBOOK

Have a place for your site visitors to make comments about the site. Ask them to sign your guestbook. This is another good way to get feedback and to meet your readers. Guest books are known for being spam magnets so make sure to include a way to know that those who sign up are real people and not robots. Use tools that will make the person sign in to eliminate the spambots.

CHAT ROOMS

Chat rooms are another way to communicate with your readers. You can host monthly chats and see your readership grow.

WORKSHOPS

You can use your site or the chat room to host workshops. On the site, there can be articles you post weekly or monthly (remember you're trying to bring the readers back). Or you can hold live chats inside your chat room.

BOOKSTORE

Always have a page that features your books and a way for readers to purchase them, either from you (autographed, of course) or through an online store. Visitors always want to buy the book after reading an excerpt. You want them to buy your book, so don't forget to offer them a chance to do so.

PODCASTS OR VIDEOS

Showcase your podcasts or videos on your site.

COUNTER

You might want to add a counter to see how many people visit your site.

RESOURCE PAGE

The resource page is a page that features links to other sites you like or links to resource sites you use for your writing. Some readers like to know about the creative side of your writing. If you do a lot of research, this is the page to include the information you found.

BLOGGING

If you choose to use a blog instead of a web page, most of the above features will work well with it.

I recommend a blog instead of a web page because it's more interactive. If you don't have time to be consistent when it comes to blogging, then stick with the website.

However, if a blog is something you want to do, sit down and create a content calendar for your blog, so you can stay consistent and you will build your readership.

A content calendar will keep you current on what content you will be sharing on your blog. You can create a separate calendar, or use the calendar you have for your promotion. I suggest using one calendar. That way, you know where everything is.

A lot of people have problems with blogs because they don't determine how often they will blog. I will admit I was guilty of this with my personal blog. With SORMAG, I knew I wanted to have content for five days. Once I realized this worked well for personal blogs, too, I was able to set up and work with a content calendar.

Consistency is the key to good blogging. Readers will return to your blog if they know they will have some new, good content to read. If the content is what they want to read, they will become loyal readers and hopefully tell others about your blog.

Scheduling your content will help you stay consistent and keep you from overwhelming yourself.

1. Decide how often you will blog.
2. Will you have a theme for your blog?
3. Will you use other people's content or create all content?
4. Schedule your content.

Now that wasn't hard; it just takes time and effort.

NOW WHAT?

You have your website/blog, now you want to know what to do next? You can wait and see how many people find you or you can invite them to your site. How do you invite them? By hosting a few activities: chats, workshops and contests.

CHATS

You can host a chat and talk about upcoming releases, writing techniques, favorite characters, great love scenes, etc.

Maybe your book's theme is about something you think your readers would be interested in discussing. The chat room could be used for this discussion.

WORKSHOPS

You can use your site or the chat room to host workshops. You can host live workshops on topics you think would interest your readers. Or you can host a workshop using articles. You can post a different article daily or weekly that discusses a specific topic. This can be very interactive if you're using a blog.

CONTESTS

Contests are a great way to bring people to your site. Everybody loves to win something. You can host monthly contests, asking readers to visit your site or sign up with your mailing list. Feature a contest each month and you'll have visitors every month. Before you host a contest, decide what you want from your visitors. This will determine what you do and how often you do it.

1. Are you trying to build up your database?
2. Are you trying to introduce new people to your book?
3. Are you just trying to have people visit and know you exist?

BUILDING UP YOUR MAILING LIST *

For this contest, you want a prize to bring people to the site, and a form for them to fill out for the contest. (Make sure you let them know that they are signing up for your database with their entry.) Set up a time frame for how long your contest will run. Always include a disclaimer stating that you're not collecting addresses to sell. Offer a freebie (an excerpt or short story) for the readers who stop by your site and sign up to your mailing list.

You will learn more about your mailing list in the next lesson.

INTRODUCE READERS TO YOUR BOOK

You can introduce your book by hosting a contest. What you give as a prize will depend on your budget. Here are a few ideas for contest prizes:

- An autographed copy of your book
- A theme, goody-filled basket
- A trip
- Gift certificates

HAVE PEOPLE VISIT AND KNOW YOU EXIST

You want people to know you exist. Offer freebies as a way to draw readers to your site. You can give away:

- Book excerpts
- Bookmarks
- Book covers
- Articles

Remember promotion is what you make of it. If you don't tell anyone about your site, don't expect to have many visitors. Just because you build it doesn't mean they will come. Tell people about your site and they'll tell people and they'll tell people.

CTION PLAN

LaShaunda's Tip

Blogging is a good way to interact with your readers. You don't have to blog every day, but you do have to be consistent. Readers want to know when they can drop by and read your latest post. Choose when you want to blog and stick to it.

Getting Started
- Keep your website current at all times.
- What's in your budget for a website/blog?
- What works best for your website/blog?
- Can you pay someone to create a website or blog?
- Can you do it yourself?
- Can you secure your domain?
- Can you secure website hosting?

- Add your website address to your marketing material and email signature.
- Do you want to host a chat?
- Do you want to write an article about the theme of your book?
- Do you want to host a contest?
- Do you want to host a workshop?
- Do you want to introduce your characters?

Checklist—Before Going Live

____ Email List (link or form)
____ Contact Me (link or form)
____ Bio/About Me
____ Articles
____ Newsletter (sign up link/form)
____ Newsletter (latest issue)
____ Media Kit
____ Bookstore
____ Does your business card and signature include your web address?

Schedule Your Calendar

- Pick a day and set an actual time you can sit down to decide what your website/blog will look like and what features you want.
- Schedule dates to write blog content.
- Schedule dates for blog updates.
- Set a date for monthly management.
- Schedule time on your calendar for the next lesson— Database/Email List.

Promotion Plan
YEARLY
- Register your domain.
- Pay for your hosting.
- Update your site/blog.
- How often will you post on your blog?
- Create content calendar.

MONTHLY
- Create content for blog posts.
- Create content for website.
- Check visitor count.
- Add content to site.

WEEKLY
- Add content to blog.
- Create social media posts (blog posts, invite to join newsletter, to join mailing list, to check out new book).
- Schedule promotion posts about blog/website.

DAILY
- Check blog for comments.
- Answer comments or questions.

HOW TO USE WEBSITE/BLOG FOR PROMOTION

- Signature—Add your website address to your signature.
- Business cards—Add your website address to your business cards.
- Email/database—Inform your friends and family members about your new site. Invite them to visit.
- Search Engines—List your site in the top search engines.

- Ask your friends if they will swap links on their sites.
- Link your site to online directories.
- Write articles and include your website link in your bio.
- Host a video blog series.
- Feature your book trailer.
- Write a series about why you started to write.
- Feature your favorite authors for the month.
- Host a contest.
- Host a blog tour.

Database/Email List

Do you have a database or email list?

Creating a database/email list is the third most important thing you do as a writer. You probably started with your email services, saving the emails you received. This is a good way to start. However, eventually you will have to create a spreadsheet or pay a database service to keep all your information. I suggest you do both. You always want to have all your readers' information.

A few email management systems are free to use for the first five hundred contacts, but will charge a fee for one thousand or more. Do your research and find the one that fits your budget. Ask your writer friends which ones they use. Which one is user friendly?

To promote your email list, include a link or form to join your list on your website/blog. You want readers to opt-in instead of you adding them to the list. If you do add them, make sure they know you are adding them to your mailing list. You don't want them to accuse you of spamming them. You want happy readers.

Your mailing list is your #3 promotion tool.
1. It can introduce you to new readers.
2. It can keep current readers informed.

3. You know who your readers are and how to reach them.
4. You own this list, which is very important.

A lot of writers rely on outside sites to gather their readers (Facebook, Twitter, Goodreads, etc.). These are all necessary sites when it comes to promotion. However, if that site were to shut down tomorrow, how would you get in touch with all your followers?

This is why it is important to have your own mailing list. You want to be able to get in touch with your followers at all times.

How you create your mailing list is up to you. Back in the day, I had mine on my Yahoo! email. When my mailing list grew larger, Yahoo! kicked me out of my account because it thought I was spamming. So I started investigating email management systems. I decided on Constant Contact. However, there are many more out there like (icontact, aweber, Mailchimp, or Mad Mimi).

This is where your friend, the search engine, comes in handy. Do your research and find the system that fits into your budget. Don't be intimidated by the various rates. Some offer free services until you build your list. Remember, you're not going to start with a list that has one thousand members on it. You begin low and work your way up. Hopefully by the time you have reached ten thousand, you're making the kind of money to pay for the services you need.

MY EXPERIENCE

My biggest mistake with creating SORMAG was not starting a mailing list. We had so many visitors the first year it was amazing. I wanted to kick myself for not capturing their names and emails. Once I learned how important it is to capture the people who visit your site, I made it my business to tell others so they don't make the same mistake.

Your mailing lists are your pot of gold. When a reader gives you their email, it means they trust you enough to come into their world. Treasure your mailing list even if you have twenty people on it right now. Those twenty people want to hear from you, which is something not many people can say.

Make sure to maintain your mailing list. Check the email address yearly. Emails change so you want to make sure you have correct emails and are not being charged for emails that no longer exist.

ACTION PLAN

LaShaunda's Tip

Don't drive yourself crazy with trying to build your list. Let it grow naturally. You want the readers who want to hear from you to join your list. They will open your emails and read them.

One thing I suggest is you break your mailing list into groups. For instance, you might have readers who are local. Create a group for them. You might have a group that only like ebooks or printed books.

Having these separate groups will save you a lot of headache in the future. You know which group to send your messages to, and you won't have to send out mass messages to your whole mailing list.

Getting Started

I use Constant Contact because I find it very user friendly. However, others offer free and paid services. If you're getting started with a small list, you might want to try out the free services first to get a feel for it. But also make sure their paid services fit into your budget.

Here are a few to get you started in your research:
* www.constantcontact.com
* www.icontact.com
* www.mailchimp.com
* www.getresponse.com
* www.aweber.com

In your favorite search engine, look up database management systems or email marketing systems.

* What services do they offer?
* How much do they charge?
* Do they offer a free service?
* Is it user friendly?
* Do they offer opt-in services (you want your readers to opt-in)?

Each service is different, so schedule time to learn your new system. I recommend you find one that has its own templates. It saves you time when it comes to creating promotional emails. All you have to do is cut and paste your content in and push SEND.

If you've been writing for a while, you might surprise yourself with the database of names and emails you already have.

Add these names and emails to your new system. Create your first email and let your friends/family/fans know why they are receiving this email—that you started a mailing list and you've included them. If they don't want to receive emails from you, they have the option to unsubscribe. Make sure you include a way to unsubscribe.

If you're on social media, send out a link to subscribe to your mailing list. (Most systems will create a link for sending out to emails, social media and for adding to your website/blog.)

How do you start your mailing list? If you are using a service, create an email and invite your friends and family. Ask them to join your list. Send out the same invite to your social media followers.

Include a link to the mailing list in your articles or blog posts you write. You can ask members who are on your mailing list to invite their friends to join your mailing list.

Include an opt-in form on your blog/site for new readers to sign up when they visit your blog/site.

When you go to conferences or literary events, bring a sign-up sheet or book and have the readers to sign up. Let them know they are being added to your mailing list. You don't want to be accused of spamming.

Building your email list is a day-by-day function. It takes time, so don't get discouraged. Be excited for the new members that sign up, and don't take it personal when someone unsubscribes. Unsubscribers mean they weren't the readers you were looking for. It's best to have a mailing list of two hundred readers who love your books than a list of one thousand readers who never buy your books.

Schedule Your Calendar
- Schedule a date to research email management systems.
- Schedule a date to create your list.
- Schedule a date to update your website/blog to feature a form to join your list.
- Schedule a date to send out your first email letter.
- Schedule a date to send out links to your email list to your social media.
- Schedule a monthly date to maintain your list.
- Schedule time on your calendar for the next lesson—Articles.

Promotion Plan
YEARLY

- Pay for email management system.
- Update your site/blog with opt-in sign up form.
- Create separate lists for (fans, book clubs, industry, states, etc.).
- Create a letter to invite your friends/fans to your mailing list.
- Create welcome letter for new members.

MONTHLY

- Maintain your list by checking bounced emails and removing invalid emails.
- Send out monthly emails if you don't have a newsletter.
- Check to see if your mailing list is growing.

WEEKLY
- Invite your social media to join your mailing list.

HOW TO USE YOUR MAILING LIST FOR PROMOTION

I use my mailing list to introduce readers to writers by sending out eblasts and newsletters. You can do the same thing.

1. You can create and send out an eblast to introduce your new book.
2. You can create a monthly newsletter.
3. You can create eblasts for monthly sales.
4. You can host contests.
5. You can host workshops.

Articles

Have you created at least six articles that
focus on your book's theme?

This lesson is a little time consuming, but once you've completed this step you will be able to use them repeatedly.

Did you know that articles are a great way to promote you and your book online? Many online magazines, sites or blogs are always looking for new submissions. They always feature a byline and a short bio. This is an excellent way to share your knowledge with readers. It will also introduce your writing abilities and place your name in the minds of readers. Some sites pay you for your articles so you can make a little money to add to your promotion budget.

I'm sure you're wondering what you can write about. You can write about your experience as a writer, the craft of writing, or maybe you're an expert in a subject. Write an article about it.

I recommend you create at least six to twelve articles, five hundred to eight hundred words each. Take the time and do this because once you get on deadline, the last thing you want to do is write an article.

If you're blogging you might have content you can reuse. Reusing content saves time and you have content when you need it.

Look at your most popular posts on your blog. Those are where you want to concentrate on topics for articles.

MY EXPERIENCE

Articles are one way I promote SORMAG without having to pitch SORMAG. I include my link in my bio with every article I write. Readers usually click on the link to learn more about the magazine.

Articles are forever and I've had readers contact me from an article I wrote years ago.

CTION PLAN

LaShaunda's Tip
Writing articles in batches is a good way to build up your stack of articles. Pick a day and write a couple of articles.

Getting Started
Here are few article ideas to get your creative juices flowing.

- What happens after the sale?
- Your favorite books on writing.
- How I stay motivated.
- Why should you buy my new book?

- How to go from story idea to manuscript.
- How to survive a writer's conference.
- Ten things to do before your book releases.
- To blog or not to blog.
- Where do my ideas come from?
- My first sale.
- Tips on writing.
- How to make the most of a critique group.

If you have a blog, look through your posts and find the top ten posts.

Look at your Facebook feed and find the top ten posts.

Have you ever written a series or article for your blog or other blogs?

Schedule Your Calendar

- Schedule time on your calendar for brainstorming by thinking up twelve ideas you want to write about.
- Schedule time on your calendar to write the articles, and create twelve Articles from these ideas.
- Schedule time on your calendar for the next lesson—Submitting Articles.

Promotion Plan
YEARLY

- How many articles will you write for the year?
- What are the topics?
- Where will you post them?
- Create an article calendar.

MONTHLY
- Schedule which month you will write articles.
- Schedule dates to write.

WEEKLY
- Write articles.
- Schedule articles on blog/site.
- Post link to social media promoting articles.

DAILY
- Check comments about articles on blog.

HOW TO USE ARTICLES
FOR PROMOTION

- Create a series with your articles.

- Pitch your series to a website/magazine or showcase on your blog/website.

- Post a monthly article on your site.

- Feature an article in your newsletter.

- Ask a writer friend if you can feature your article in their newsletter or on their website/blog.

- Feature your articles in an article directory.

Submitting Articles

Have you submitted the articles you created?

BEFORE YOU BEGIN

- Remember to do your research first.

- Check out the online magazines/sites/blogs to see if their readerships are the readers you want to reach.

- See what types of articles these online magazines/sites/blogs are looking for because you don't want to submit a medical article to a poetry magazine.

- Some online magazines/sites/ blogs have a writing calendar with the themes for the year, which can help you in knowing what to offer as an article.

- What is the word count? This will help you when you begin to write your articles.

- Whom do you submit to? I highly recommend knowing the name of the editor.

- How do they want you to submit? Read over their guidelines. Do not send your article without permission.

LET'S CONNECT

A letter of introduction is a way to introduce you and your book to online magazines/sites/blogs. You're offering your services to them and in return, they let you know if they can use your services. I recommend including the editor/publisher's name (make sure you spell it correctly). It lets them know you have done your research. You're trying to stand out, not get deleted.

BIOS

When you submit your articles, the publication will also want a short bio on you of twenty-five words or less. This is similar to your signature, with a little more information about yourself. Make sure to have a link to your site. Include a picture of you, your book and a short synopsis of the book. You want to provide everything needed when you submit your article. You don't want them having to search for your information.

COLUMNIST

Another option is becoming a columnist for an online magazine/site/blog. This is your chance to talk about the special topic only you know about. Share your wisdom with their readership and at the end of your column, include your bio. If you're lucky, some sites pay for content.

Before you commit to being a columnist, make sure you have the time to commit to writing your column. It sounds great to have your own column, but if you're on deadline, the last thing you want to think about is that eight-hundred-word column that is due in two days.

Check out your favorite online magazines/sites/blogs to see if they're in need of a columnist and send an introduction letter to the editor and offer your services.

You have your articles, your bio, and you're ready to send out your letters of introduction. Remember your purpose for the submission is to introduce yourself to their readers.

I recommend using this tool off the net, too.

MY EXPERIENCE

Submitting an article isn't hard, but I will be the first to admit that I've missed deadlines—not intentionally—because life got in the way. I apologized and asked if they still wanted the article I submitted. Things happen. If you can't submit your article, make sure to let the editor know so arrangements can be made to replace your article or wait for you. Keeping your editor posted shows your professionalism and they will be willing to work with you again.

*CA*CTION PLAN

LaShaunda's Tip
Read the guidelines for where you want to submit. You don't want to waste their time or yours by sending articles they can't use.

Getting Started
List ten sites to submit articles.

- What you need from them:
  - Email address to contact.
  - When and how they want you to contact them.

- What type of articles are they looking for (guidelines)?
- Who are their readers?
- Write your introduction letter.
- Write your bio.

SAMPLE INTRODUCTION LETTER

Dear Ms. Hampton,

This is an important part of the letter. Make sure you have the correct name.

Greetings in the name of literature. I am LaShaunda C. Hoffman. I'm currently promoting my new book and would like to introduce it to your readers. I would like to write an article for you concerning my experience in attending my first conference.

Introduce yourself and what you would like to write about.

It will be an 800-word article and will include pictures.

If this isn't something that interests you, I have a variety of subjects to discuss (relationships, Christian life, blogging, natural hair care, online marketing or about writing).

Offer another suggestion in case they might want something different.

Please let me know if you would like me to send you the article.

I look forward to working with you.

Sincerely,

LaShaunda C. Hoffman
writerlh@yahoo.com

SAMPLE BIO

LaShaunda C. Hoffman is a Christian Fiction author who enjoys reading and chatting online. Her debut novel, *Trust in the Lord*, is due out June 2015. Visit her online at http://lashaunda.blogspot.com

Schedule Your Calendar

- Pick a day and set an actual time to sit down to research the sites you want to pitch your articles to.

- Schedule dates to write articles if you don't have any written.

- Schedule a date to write your pitch letter.

- Schedule a date to send out letters.

- Keep a log on whom you sent letters to and when you sent them, and include who accepted them and who rejected them.

- Schedule time on your calendar for the next lesson—Monthly Newsletters

Promotion Plan

YEARLY—Determine how many articles you would like to submit for the year.

MONTHLY—Determine how many articles you will submit for the month.

WEEKLY—Maintain a record of articles submitted and how many were accepted or denied.

ARTICLE CHECKLIST

_____ Article title

_____ Article word count

_____ Sites to submit to

_____ Site's editor

_____ Dates articles are submitted

_____ Dates received replies

_____ Dates to follow-up on articles submitted

_____ When article(s) will be published

_____ Schedule article(s) live on your calendar

_____ Visit site(s) to see article(s)

_____ Promote article(s)

_____ Send "thank you" note, and pitch another story

Newsletters

Do you have a monthly newsletter?

A newsletter for your email list is the perfect way to get information out about your latest book, or if you're going to be at an event, you can send it out in your newsletter.

How much you want to feature in your newsletter is up to you. Keep it interesting. Add a few tidbits about you, the writer and the person. Include your book and how to purchase it. Tell them where they can meet you at literary events. Include one of the articles you've been working on. You want the reader to look forward to your newsletter each month.

The object of the newsletter is to keep your name and book in front of your readers. Remember there are millions of books every year. If they don't know about yours, they will choose someone else's. We don't want that to happen.

You always want to think about building up your database, and a newsletter is a good way to do this. Make sure to let others know about your newsletter, online and offline. Take a guestbook with you to events and ask readers to join your newsletter list by signing your guestbook with their information.

Content is king. What you put in your newsletter is what makes them open it. Make sure you have some good content featured in your newsletter, so the readers are always waiting to open it and read all your content.

Here are a few things you can feature in your newsletter.

CONTESTS

Readers like contests. Hosting a contest in your newsletter is a great way to grow your email list.

ARTICLES

Articles are another way to encourage others to sign up for your newsletter. Remember those articles you wrote? You can feature one each month and let your readers know if they sign up for your newsletter, they can expect a new article each month.

INTERVIEWS

Interview fellow authors each month, interview one of your characters or one of your readers.

Your newsletter can be something you post on your website/blog or you can send it out to your mailing list. I recommend including an opt-in link, so you can collect the names of those who are interested in reading your newsletter. The more interesting your newsletter, the more readers want to receive it.

MY EXPERIENCE

I will admit, I like newsletters, which is why I created newsletters eBlasts for SORMAG Promotions. I also do a promotion newsletter, "See Ya On The 'Net—Online Promotion Tips."

I try to keep them short and informative. I also subscribe to many author newsletters. I love learning about what they are up to and their latest books. I think newsletters are informative and a great way to keep your readers updated with what's happening in your writing world.

CTION PLAN

LaShaunda's Tip
Newsletters can be time consuming, so seriously consider if this is something you want to do and how often you want to send it out (weekly, bi-weekly, monthly, quarterly).

Getting Started
- Pick five of your favorite authors and subscribe to their newsletters.

- What is it you like about their newsletter?

- What makes you want to read their newsletters each month?

- Are there any ideas you can use for your own newsletter?

- Putting together a monthly newsletter isn't hard, but it does take time and you need different content each month. Here are few ideas to get you started:
  - Inspirational quotes
  - Books you are reading
  - Questions from readers
  - Questions for your readers
  - Pictures of events

- Book trivia
- Recipes
- Birthday listings
- Interview listings
- Contest winners
- Special events
- Where to find you online
- What's new with you
- Historical tidbits
- Story behind your novel
- Create twelve newsletter ideas
- Create six contests to host in your newsletter

Schedule Your Calendar
- Schedule time on your calendar to brainstorm your newsletter.
- Schedule time on your calendar to create your newsletter each month.
- Schedule time on your calendar for the date your newsletter will go out to your readers each month.
- Schedule time on your calendar for the next lesson—Social Media.

Promotion Plan
YEARLY
- Decide if you will send out a newsletter.
- How often will you send it out?
- What will you feature in newsletter?

MONTHLY
- Schedule date for newsletter to go out.
- Write content for newsletter.

WEEKLY
- Promote newsletter on social media.
- Ask social media followers to subscribe to newsletter.

HOW TO USE YOUR NEWSLETTER FOR PROMOTION

- Feature a contest.

- Feature Fan Of The Month.

- Introduce a character; include a picture of what you think the character looks like.

- Feature a book club you visited, include pictures of the visit.

- Spotlight a conference you attended.

Social Media

What social media are you on?

Why are you on social media? Most writers don't think about this question. Most are on social media because that's what *they* say to do. However when you join a social media platform you need to know WHY?

Answer the following questions. They will help you determine your goals for social media, then you can create a plan to help you find time to be on social media, get results from being on social media and feel as if you're getting something out of social media.

- Why are you on social media?
- What do you want to gain from social media?
- How often do you think you should be on social media?
- What do you like and dislike about social media?

I'm one of those people who like social media. Most of my time is online, so I like interacting with my friends online. I also like being able to network with people I might not ever get a chance to meet unless I was at an event. Social media lets me have fun and network all in the comfort of my home.

I recommend you pick at least two social media to participate on. Find two you enjoy because if you pick something you don't enjoy you won't deal with it. I like Twitter, but I know a few people who hate it. Social media is about networking. You have to find the networking system you like. Learn them, use them and have fun. Why two? You don't want to feel overwhelmed and your readers can be on either one of the sites and that way you are able to interact with them.

You're probably thinking you don't have time to learn something new. True, but you also need to participate on social media, too, if you're not doing a lot of networking on the outside.

You have to make time to meet new readers. This is an excellent way to interact with your readers. Remember that's your goal, building your readership.

I'm a Facebook and Twitter girl. I use Facebook for fun interaction. I talk with my readers daily. I use Twitter to learn and share. I'm forever clicking on links to great articles.

You don't have to be online all day long. Pick a time that works for you. Twice a day, once day—there is no correct amount of time. Don't be a once a month drive-by. You want to interact and not let them forget you were even on the site.

If you're not on any social media, talk with your fellow writer friends and see which ones they like. Then go out and play. Find the ones you're comfortable with and let everyone know your social media addresses. Include them on your website and all information you send out (business cards, press kits, etc.).

Remember, social media is about sharing, not selling.

Social media is also about having conversations. You want to know what people think about your book. Join reader groups and create a Fan Page on Facebook. Talk with your readers. Learn what they like or dislike about your books.

Be a part of the conversation, and you will see social media can be fun and helpful to your writing career.

What I love about social media is the content you can get from others. I've found some amazing courses to take. I've read posts about the craft and business of writing. I've learned how to create podcasts. All from content shared on social media.

Most writers are on FB and most are just joining conversations and that's fine. This is a form of networking. However, you also have to be contributing in order to bring people back to you. This is where the sharing comes in.

Social media is about sharing.

Look at your schedule and see how much time you have for social media. If you're one who doesn't have time, scheduling your content will work well for you. You will be participating in social media, but you won't have to worry about it taking up all of your time.

SCHEDULING SOCIAL MEDIA

One of the best ways to share content is to schedule your posts. I like using Hootsuite, a social media manager. I can be on social media all day and never even log in.

I pick one day of the week, usually Saturday morning or Sunday afternoon, and schedule my content for the week. For example:

- I post daily Dreams graphics that include quotes about following your dreams.

- I post daily SORMAG Tips graphics that include promotion tips.

- I post links to SORMAG eBlasts.
- I post links to my blog entries.
- I post articles I find interesting.
- I share literary news.
- I invite my followers to join my newsletter listings.

I schedule my posts so it looks like I'm online all day. Since I work a full-time job, I don't have time to be on social media during the day. However, with scheduling my content, I'm able to share and network without having to check my social media every hour.

This is my daily contribution to social media content. I love when someone shares or likes because it means they get it and they appreciate my content.

I do believe in connecting on social media, so I schedule time to respond to comments on my social media and to make comments on my followers' pages. You don't want to be one of those who only posts information, and don't communicate with those you're sending posts to or to those who respond to your posts.

For me I cut a lot of my time on social media by scheduling my time. I schedule when I will be on social media and I schedule the content I will share on social media. I wouldn't be able to participate in social media if it wasn't for my social media manager. It makes me look like I'm online all day when I'm working my full-time job.

Don't get me wrong I waste a lot of time on social media too, who doesn't. However, I try to stick to my goal of meeting new people each day.

I break up my time—forty-five minutes before work, fifteen minutes at lunch and one to two hours at night. Most times my time is at night. I have the laptop and if I'm not writing or working on SORMAG stuff, I'm on social media. I'll admit it I don't have much of a social life. The hubby works nights, so my social life is online.

If you have a social life, find what's comfortable for you. Reply to posts on your profile or FB page. Those are the most important because your readers are communicating with YOU on these pages. You don't want to be that writer that only posts and never responds.

If you are in a few groups, stop by and see what's going on. Add your comments to a few posts. Offer some advice if needed. Share some information if you have something to share.

Then if you have time, check out your feed and see what's going on in the FB community. Talk to the people, engage.

This doesn't have to take a long time. If you have a habit of getting lost on FB, set a timer and stick to it.

How often do you want to do this? I suggest daily, however I understand you might be on deadline and can't squeeze in the time, then schedule the time. Pick two days to pop in and be social. You determine which days and how much time you want be on social media. Once you get into the habit of this, it won't feel so overwhelming. It's as if you are making an appointment to hang out with your readers. When you look at social media like that, social media can be a fun time instead of something taking you away from your writing.

Scheduling your social media will make your online promotion a lot easier especially when you are on deadline and have banned yourself from social media. You can preschedule your promotion and focus on your writing.

MY EXPERIENCE

I enjoy social media. I don't have much of a social life as a full-time worker, mom and wife, so I do a lot online. I enjoy hanging out on Facebook and talking with followers. In the different groups I belong to, I meet a lot of new authors, and I have great discussions in the online book clubs. I learn a lot about writing and business from the links shared on Twitter and LinkedIn. Most of the webinars/teleseminars I learn about are from social media. To me it's one of the best places to network, share and learn.

 CTION PLAN

LaShaunda's Tip
Social media can be time consuming, so schedule your time online and stick to it if you're on a deadline.

When I'm super busy, I limit my social media to an hour. I set the clock and I visit my different social media sites. I check for replies and respond accordingly. I want to be a participant not a drive-by member.

EXAMPLE SCHEDULE

MONDAY
Facebook—Visit Reader Groups

TUESDAY
Twitter—Share content, retweet content, link articles

WEDNESDAY
Google+—share content

THURSDAY
LinkedIn—Visit writer's groups

FRIDAY
Facebook—Share content, talk with followers

SATURDAY
Pinterest—Maintain boards

Getting Started
Here are a few questions to answer:
- What social media will you focus on?
- How often would you like to be on social media?
- Will you use tools to maintain a presence on social media?
- Will you join social media groups? Which ones?
- Will you create a group for you/your book?
- Will you create a group based on a topic/theme?
- Will you use a social media management like Hootsuite or Buffer app?

Choose five social media sites:
- Facebook
- Twitter
- LinkedIn
- Pinterest
- Instagram
- MySpace
- Google+

Here's a link to a list of other social networking websites: http://en.wikipedia.org/wiki/List_of_social_networking_ websites

- What do you like about it?
- What don't you like about it?
- Choose two networks to work with.
- Use Hootsuite or another social media manager as a way to schedule your posts. This way you look like you're online all day but you're really writing.

Schedule Your Calendar
- Pick a day and set an actual time you can sit down to research, which social media you would like to use.
- Schedule dates to set up your accounts for social media.
- Schedule dates and times you will promote on social media.
- Schedule one hour each day to check out your social media sites.
- Set a date for monthly management.
- Schedule time on your calendar for the next lesson—Sites/ Blogs

Promotion Plan
YEARLY
- Decide which social media you will use for promoting this year.
- Decide if you will use a social media management site (Hootsuite or Buffer app).
- Join the social media if you are not a member.

- Create your own group.
- Create your profile pages.
- Create a social media schedule.

MONTHLY

- Create social media graphics.

- Host a monthly book discussion in your group.

- Create theme status posts (for example: What's your favorite research site?).

WEEKLY

- Visit your followers' pages.
- Ask them a question or make a comment.
- Set up your social media management for content to share.

DAILY

Check your posts for comments.

HOW TO USE SOCIAL MEDIA FOR PROMOTION

- Post inspirational quotes using the social media graphics you created.
- Create a research page on Pinterest.
- Host a Twitter chat.
- Share your expertise in a LinkedIn group.
- Host a Google hangout workshop on Google +.

There are many ways to promote using your social media and that's a whole other book. I've included a few tips in the workbook.

Sites/Blogs

Have you researched the sites/blogs that promote your genre?

Now that you have the website every reader wants to visit, you can move on to letting more readers know about you and your book. A good place to start is by visiting other sites and blogs.

If you've been online for a while, you're probably doing this already. You have your favorite sites and blogs you visit daily or monthly. You might even be on the RSS Feeds so you can receive their posts in your email account.

INTERACT

One of the best parts about blogs and social media is the interaction. You can meet tons of readers by interacting on blogs or social media.

Visit blogs/social media and make comments on the posts that interest you. Engage with the readers. Don't do drive-by posts. Be a real visitor who enjoys the blog you visit.

I've met a lot of writers by visiting their blogs or blogs they have visited and commented on them. Readers like to know what you think about things and if you include a link to your blog/website, they will follow your link.

GUEST BLOGGING

Being the featured guest on someone's blog is a good way to meet their readers. You can be the featured author for the day, or you can write an article or talk about a topic.

If you did the article assignment then you have your articles you can pitch to be a guest.

TOPICS

Your next assignment is to create ten topics you can talk about. If your book has a theme, this is the perfect way to discuss it. Do you have a hidden talent? If so, write about it.

Here are a few examples to get you started.

1. How I made my first sale.
2. Why I chose to self-publish instead of traditional publishing.
3. How to market your ebook.
4. Why is a writer's organization important?
5. How to network at a conference.

See how different these topics are? Consider what would interest readers and writers, and write a five hundred to one-thousand-word article on it. Place these articles in a folder for future use. (If you completed LESSON: ARTICLES then you already have these done, so you're ready to move forward.)

WRITE AN INTRODUCTION LETTER

You've visited a few sites and blogs and you like the atmosphere on them and think your book would be perfect to introduce to its readership. Now it's time to do an introduction letter to the site/blog. I recommend sending your letter of introduction three to six months before your book releases. You want to give the site/blog hosts time to schedule you on their calendars. Waiting until the week your book releases is not a good idea.

EXAMPLE INTRODUCTION LETTER

Hello (name of site/blog host):

How are you today?

My name is LaShaunda Hoffman and I am the author of the new book, *Destiny*. It is a historical romance set in Asheville, North Carolina. It will be released in December 2014.

As a fan of your site/blog, I would like to be featured on it. I'm available for an interview, chat or I can write an article.

I hope we can work together in the future. I look forward to hearing from you.

I can be reached at: sormag@yahoo.com or http://lashaunda.blogspot.com

Sincerely,

LaShaunda C. Hoffman
writerlh@yahoo.com

MY EXPERIENCE

When I started SORMAG, blogs and sites were how I met authors and readers. There wasn't social media, so I had to visit a lot of sites and blogs. I found a few I enjoyed and visited often and interacted with the others who visited. Don't be a lurker if you plan to pitch articles, blog/site hosts like familiarity. If they are familiar with you, they'll tend to work with you. Interact with the blog/site and you'll learn about it and what the hosts like in their posts.

# CTION PLAN

LaShaunda's Tip
Visit the sites/blogs before you send your letters. Get to know the readers and the host. Participate in the conversation. Approach them after you get a feel for the site/blog.

Getting Started
• Write down five friends who are online with either a site or blog.

• Write down five websites you visit frequently.

• Write down five blogs you visit frequently. (Do not repeat any from previous lists.)

• Find five places that promote your genre.

Now you have twenty places to visit. That wasn't so hard, was it? If you have more sites and blogs that you visit, that's good because you want to build up the places you visit. For now though, let's stick to twenty to get your feet wet. Remember there is no guarantee that all twenty sites/blogs will say yes, however if you present yourself professionally, you have a better chance of them saying yes.

For the list you created, below is the information you will need from each site:

- Name of host.

- Email address to contact.

- When and how they want you to contact them (interviews, articles, book reviews and chats).

- What genre they promote? (If they don't promote your genre, do not contact.)

- Who are their readers?

- Is there a charge for promotion? If so, what are their prices?

Next, write your introduction letter and send it out to the twenty sites.

Schedule Your Calendar
- Schedule a day and set an actual time you can sit down to research sites and blogs that promote your genre. Don't skimp on this time. This is one lesson you will continue throughout your writing career. For each book, you will need to make time to research new sites/blogs to be featured on.

- Schedule a date to write a letter of introduction.

- Keep a log of the places you visit.

- Schedule time on your calendar for the next lesson—Blog Tours.

Promotion Plan
YEARLY
Research sites/blogs, and find those that cater to your niche. You will do this for each book you write because you want to find new sites/blogs to promote on each year.

MONTHLY
- Schedule dates to visit the site/blog. Get to know it and its readers.
- Write a letter of introduction to site/blog.
- Write content for guest blogs.

WEEKLY
- Promote any scheduled interview or guest blogging on your social media.
- Include information in your newsletter and on your blog/website.
- Visit sites that host you.
- Answer any questions or comments.

HOW TO USE SITE/BLOG
FOR PROMOTION

- Pitch writing about researching your book (as guest blogger or article).
- Schedule interviews with site/blog.
- Guest blogger—answer questions about writing or a specific topic.

- Host a live chat.

- Host an excerpt contest, where readers are to locate a quote in your excerpt.

Blog Tours

Have you decided if you would do a blog tour?

A blog tour is asking different sites/blogs to host you for the day. If you did LESSON: SITES/BLOGS, you began the process of setting up the blog tour. You have your sites/blogs you want to visit. Now you have to set a date for your tour and send out a letter requesting to be hosted on your specific dates.

A blog tour can be a fun way to introduce your book to readers. Unfortunately, a lot of authors have treated their blog tour like a one-day advertisement instead of a book tour.

With a book tour, you can't sign books if you don't show up. I've found that many authors aren't showing up for their own blog tours. Doesn't sound very professional, does it? It's not; however many authors schedule blog tours and think all they have to do is send a blurb about their book and a canned interview and BAM they're on tour. If all you want is a one-day promo, pay for a one-day promotion and don't call it a tour.

A real blog tour takes time and commitment if you treat it like a real book tour. If you don't have time, don't sign up for one. Enough with my fussing.

As one who enjoys a good blog tour, I want to offer a few tips to help you have a successful one.

Before I begin, please note that a blog tour does not equate to SALES, but a way to introduce you and your book to new readers. If you do sell a couple of books because of the tour, count it as a blessing.

1. **KNOW YOUR SCHEDULE**—Can you do a one-week, two-week or one-month tour? You need to be available to follow your tour. If you're on deadline, this is not the time to schedule a tour. Don't overbook yourself. Yes you have a one-week tour, but you have five stops per day. Can you handle five sites per day? That's a lot of typing if you have readers asking you questions. Make sure you can handle the typing commitment it might take to tour on certain sites.

2. **SHARE SOMETHING DIFFERENT**—Make sure each stop has something different to post. Some readers like to follow the tours, and they like to read different posts. Don't have the same thing posted at every site—that makes for a boring tour. Be creative; make your tour about you and the book. Entice the reader to want more.

3. **PROMOTE YOUR TOUR**—If you don't tell your readers about the tour, how will they know? Post the schedule on your site/blog. Send a post to your social media. Promote, promote, promote.

4. **GIVEAWAYS**—Readers love winning prizes. Think of fun things to give away: gift certificates, gift baskets, backlist of your books. Don't forget to let the readers know in your promotion that you will be giving away prizes.

5. **VISIT YOUR TOUR**—Make time each day of the tour to visit the site hosting you. Stop by the site and thank the person hosting the tour. Answer any questions or comments left in the comment section. Don't get discouraged if no one leaves a comment or question. Many readers read the posts, but don't comment. If you want to interact with the readers, let them know when you will visit the site and show up at that time, for a Q&A session.

6. **GIVEAWAY SUGGESTIONS**—Host a giveaway for the hosts with the most comments. Hosts love a little competition to see if they can get the most comments.

   • Offer a prize to the reader who follows you on your tour. Readers like following the tour. Have them post a comment at each stop and draw a name from the readers who participate.

   • Offer a prize for joining your newsletter. You're always working on building your mailing list with new readers. Offer a chance to readers at each site to join your newsletter. Maybe tempt them with an excerpt for your next book.

7. **REMEMBER TO HAVE FUN**—You want to be able to do this again. If it is so time consuming that you're not having fun meeting new readers, you won't want to do it again. Have fun.

8. **STOP BY THE SITE AGAIN**—After the tour is done, stop by each site to make sure you answered all the comments/questions and say "thank you" again to the host.

9. **SEND OUT PRIZES**—Make sure you send out your prizes in a timely manner. You don't want your winners contacting the hosts for their prizes.

10. EVALUATE YOUR TOUR

- How did the tour go?

- Did you have any comments?

- Did you meet any readers?

- Is this something you want to do for future books?

- Did you get new readers to join your mailing list?

- Did you sell any books?

Sounds like a lot of work, doesn't it? It can be and that's why you should schedule your tour when you have the time and the commitment to tour. The goal of a blog tour is to meet new readers. You want to make a lasting impression on them. Make them feel as if they attended a live book tour. They will remember your name and your book, and hopefully they will buy a copy and tell their friends about it.

There a few companies who can help you create an online book tour, if you don't want to do the work. Below are a few to get you started:

Write Now Literary Virtual Blog Tours
http://wnlbooktours.com/

Pump Up Your Book
http://www.pumpupyourbook.com

Tywebbin Creations
http://tywebbincreations.com/

Christian Fiction Alliance
http://www.christianfictionblogalliance.com/services.html

MY EXPERIENCE

I enjoy a good blog tour. One of my favorites was a tour done by Christian writer Angela Benson. She writes Christian romance and she had a blog tour of thirty sites, one site a day for thirty days. It was a fun tour. I visited each site because each site had different content. Angela also made time to visit each site and answer questions and mingled with readers. She made it fun and it was a tour I will always remember. Make your blog tour a fun experience for those who visit it.

CTION PLAN

LaShaunda's Tip
Be unique with your blog tour. Don't follow what everyone else is doing. Show the readers something different, so they remember your book.

Getting Started
- Create a list of sites to visit (five to ten sites)
- What you need to know
- Email address to contact
- When and how they want you to contact them

- What genre they promote
- Who are their readers
- Write a letter requesting they host your blog tour

Below are **four blogs to get you started:**

http://sormag.blogspot.com
http://www.writtenvoicesblog.com/
http://readinnwritin.blogspot.com/
http://conversationslive.blogspot.com/

SAMPLE BLOG TOUR LETTER

Hello (name of site/blog host):

My name is LaShaunda Hoffman. I would like for your blog to be a stop on my blog tour I'm hosting in May. I have the following dates *(example: 5/5, 5/6, 5/9, 5/12)* available.

If this sounds like something you would like to participate in, please let me know what date works for you and I will send you the content needed for the blog.

As a host, I would like to offer you a PDF copy of my new book, *Destiny*. It is a historical romance set in Asheville, North Carolina.

I hope we can work together. I look forward to hearing from you.

I can be reached at: sormag@yahoo.com or http://lashaunda. blogspot.com.

Sincerely,

LaShaunda C. Hoffman

CHECKLIST FOR BLOG TOUR

_____	Blog tour dates
_____	Blog tour letter
_____	Blog tour sites
_____	Blog tour content
_____	Promote the tour
_____	Visit the tour
_____	Prizes for tour
_____	Social media promotion
_____	Promotion graphics
_____	Thank you letter for after tour
_____	Send out prizes

Schedule Your Calendar

- Pick a day and set an actual time you can sit down to decide if you want to do a blog tour and when you want the tour to run.

- Schedule a date to write blog tour request letter.

- Schedule dates for blog tour.

- Schedule dates to write blog tour content and marketing material.

- Schedule dates for blog tour.

- Schedule date to write thank you note for blog tour hosts.

- Schedule date to mail off blog tour prizes.

- Keep a log of the blogs you send letters to and the blogs you choose to tour.

- Schedule time on your calendar for the next lesson— FORUMS/GROUPS/LISTS.

Promotion Plan
YEARLY
- Decide if you are hosting a blog tour this year.
- How many?
- Will you set it up yourself or pay for a service?

MONTHLY
- Visit blogs you are interested in touring.
- Create a tour letter.
- Create promo material and content for tour.
- Send tour content to blogs.

WEEKLY
- Promote tour on social media (schedule posts).
- Promote tour on your site/blog.
- Promote in newsletter.

DAILY
- Visit each stop on the tour.
- Answer any questions or comments.
- Thank the host for hosting you.

HOW TO USE BLOG TOURS FOR PROMOTION

- Feature your book trailer as part of the tour content.

- Feature a chapter excerpt as part of the tour content.

- Create a special gift basket based on your book's theme as a prize for the tour. Only those who attend the tour and leave a comment can be entered into the contest.

- Create special promotion material for the tour and post it on all social media and in your newsletter.

Forums/Groups/ Lists 16

Have you researched forums/groups/lists that promote your genre?

Now it's time to do a little more networking. Your goal is to introduce new readers to your new book and your website. A good place for this is by visiting readers/writer forums/groups/lists.

FORUMS/GROUPS/LISTS

Forums are message boards where you can post messages. Groups are rooms on social media (they can be private or open). Lists are usually emails that come as individual emails or digest forms.

Readers love forums/groups/lists especially if they can discuss their favorite topic—books. If you plan to join a few forums/lists, read their rules first. Many forums/groups/lists hate for writers to join just to announce their books. Be a real, active member. This will let the members of the forums/groups/lists know you're part of the group's membership and not just using the forums/

groups/lists as an advertising tool.

This is the place to exercise your signature. Make sure that every time you make a post or send an email you have your signature at the bottom. Don't forget to check their signature rules.

What I like about forums and lists is all the expertise. I can post a question and I know someone will take a moment to answer it. You can be that person who answers the question. Share your knowledge. Members will remember and when your book comes out, they will pick it up and recommend it to others.

BOOK DISCUSSION

Online is a great way to do book discussions. They can be held on forums, groups, lists and chat rooms. Contact the forums/lists and see if they're interested in discussing your book.

One forum I belonged to had deep discussions about current books. It's even more interesting if the author is participating in the discussions. The readers are able to ask them about the book, the characters, the plot and they can answer these questions.

After the discussion, ask the participants to post reviews on Amazon.com. No fake reviews. Readers can spot them a mile away.

CHAT ROOMS

Many forums have chat rooms and you can take advantage of this by being a guest for a chat. For example, a forum I managed used to host monthly chats with authors. The authors discussed their books and answered questions from those attending the chat.

One of the most memorable chats I attended was with Rochelle Alers. We were discussing her book *Vows*, sharing our thoughts on the book and the hero, Joshua. Years later, the people who attended this chat are still talking about it. That's what you want people to do…talk about your book.

LETTER OF INTRODUCTION

You don't have to join a forum/group/list to participate in them. When I was a member of RWA (Romance Writers Of America), the list I belonged to hosted monthly craft workshops. They invited different authors to talk about different parts of writing. This could be you.

Send a letter of introduction to see if they would like to feature you on forums/groups/lists. Some social media groups offer Featured Author For The Day. You could be that featured author. You have a chance to meet the members for the day and talk about you, your writing and your book.

MY EXPERIENCE

Forums are where I got my introduction to online promotion. I belong to Delphiforums.com, a site dedicated to forums of all topics of discussion. I wanted to meet other writers so I created Aspiring African American Romance Writers. This forum is no longer active, however this is where my lessons on promotion began. It was a day-by-day process. I learned something new every day. The best part for me was keeping an open mind and trying new things. It's the only way to meet new readers.

Be the expert. Forums/groups/lists are the perfect place for you to be the expert. Share your experience about the writing business or whatever topic you are knowledgeable. Be part of the forums/groups/lists. Readers remember your being a member versus your being a promoter. Some of my best networking has been inside of forums/groups/lists.

Inside forums/groups/lists, I learned about literary events, literary news or the writing business. I kept current on what was happening in the literary world. Don't miss out on networking this way. The best part is you never leave your home.

CTION PLAN

LaShaunda's Tip
Create your own group for your readers. Post weekly posts and host monthly meetings. Interact with your readers…get to know them.

Getting Started
Promoting on forums/groups/lists is a great way to network, and meet new readers and writers who just might introduce you to other readers, writers and sites. Find forums/groups/lists on Yahoo.com, Delphiforums.com, Msn.com and Aol.com, and most social media sites, just to name a few. Search for the forum/groups/lists that represent the genre in which you write.

I also suggest you check out your organization affiliations (professional, writing, etc.). Many have forums/groups/lists online. Make sure you join them, too. Or see if they will feature you.

What you need:
- Name of host.

- Contact's email address.

- When and how they want to be contacted.
- What type of topics are they looking for (guidelines)?
- Who are their readers?
- What topics would you like to pitch?
- Write your introduction letter.

SAMPLE INTRODUCTION LETTER

Greetings in the name of literature,

I hope life is treating you wonderfully.

My name is LaShaunda C. Hoffman. I'm currently promoting my new book and would like to introduce it to your forum members. I'm available to host workshops or chats. I have a variety of subjects to discuss (relationships, Christian life, blogging, natural hair care, online marketing or about writing), or we can discuss my book.

If this sounds like something you would like to do, please reply to this message.

I look forward to working with you.

Sincerely,

LaShaunda C. Hoffman
writerlh@yahoo.com

Schedule Your Calendar
- Schedule a day and set an actual time you can sit down to research forums/groups/lists that promote your genre. Don't

skimp on this time. Again, this is a lesson you will continue to use throughout your writing career.

- For each book, you need to make time to research new forums/groups/lists for networking.
- Schedule dates and time to visit the forums/groups/lists to see if you would like to participate in them.
- Schedule a date to write introduction letters.
- Schedule a date to send introduction letters.
- Schedule time on your calendar for the next lesson—Online Book Clubs.

Promotion Plan

- Research forums/groups/list to find those that cater to your niche.
- You will do this for each book you write. You want to make sure these groups are current each year.
- Join a few groups that interest you and be an active participant.
- Decide if you want to host workshops, chats or book discussions.

MONTHLY

- Schedule dates to visit forums/groups/lists.
- Send out letters to forums/groups/lists.
- Schedule workshops/chats or book discussions.

WEEKLY

- Visit forums/groups/lists.
- Be the expert, answer questions.

DAILY

- On the day of your workshop/chat/discussion, make sure to show up on time.

- Present your workshop.

- Answer questions and comments.

HOW TO USE FOR PROMOTION

- Be an expert
- Host chats
- Host a workshop
- Q&A session
- Host a contest
- Book discussion

The best way you can promote in forums/groups/lists is to be an active participant. Become one of the best members. As a member, they might offer times where writers can promote their books. Don't miss out on this opportunity.

Learn what the readers like in this group. Don't be a drive-by member.

Online Book
Clubs

Have you researched online book clubs?

ONLINE BOOK CLUBS

Online book clubs are similar to live book clubs; they feature authors and their books. Some even let you discuss the book with the members. Others might feature excerpts of your book.

Contact your writer friends and see which online book clubs they deal with, and do a Google search for online book clubs. Look up book clubs that read your genre. Read their guidelines carefully. You want to know how to submit your book. Don't send your book without prior notice. Stay on their good side. You don't want to send your book to someone who doesn't read your genre.

Be a member of a book club. Every good writer reads. Join a few book clubs. Become a good member. You don't have to promote your book. Most times a member will ask you about your book. Sometimes book clubs will select your book for the monthly selection. Even if they don't select your books, read the books they select, participate in the group discussions and interact with the members.

LETTER OF INTRODUCTION

After doing your research, now you're ready to introduce yourself to the book clubs. Send out your emails and offer your services for a book discussion or chat with an author.

CHATS

You can do chats online in chat rooms, over the phone or via Skype. (Never skyped before? Talk with your fellow authors for their advice or do a Google search and see what you're missing).

SORMAG's Ereader Book Club is a group on Facebook. We post questions as our book discussion. You can do the same for other groups, lists or forums. Do what makes you feel comfortable and remember to have fun.

MY EXPERIENCE

Social media is an ideal place for online book clubs. I belong to four online book clubs and I host a book club. In SORMAG's Ereader Book Club, we read one book a month. Sometimes we invite the author to stop by and participate in the discussion. Since we are all on different time zones, our monthly meeting is set for the entire day. I post questions and members stop by when they can to answer the questions.

 CTION PLAN

LaShaunda's Tip

Create your own book club. Read your book and other writers' books. Have book discussions once a month. Let your members recommend books to read. Have fun reading books.

Getting Started

What you need to know:

- Name of host.

- Contact's email address.

- When and how they want to be contacted.

- What type of books are they looking for (guidelines)?

- Who are their readers?

- What topics would you like to pitch?

- Write your introduction letter.

EXAMPLE LETTER

Greetings in the name of literature,

My name is LaShaunda C. Hoffman.

I'm currently promoting my new book and would like to introduce it to your book club. My book is a historical romance set in Asheville, North Carolina.

I hope this is something your book club might be interested in reading. If you'd like, I'd be happy to send you a review copy.

Please let me know if you would like to set up a book discussion or chat with me.

I look forward to working with you.

LaShaunda C. Hoffman
writerlh@yahoo.com

Schedule Your Calendar

- Schedule a day and set an actual time you can sit down to research online book clubs that promote your genre. Don't skimp on this time. Again, this is a lesson you will continue to use throughout your writing career.

- Schedule dates and time to visit the book clubs to see if you would like to participate in them.

- Schedule a date to write introduction letters.

- Schedule a date to send introduction letters.

- Schedule time on your calendar for the next lesson—Online Radio.

Promotion Plan
YEARLY

- Research online book clubs and find those that cater to your niche.

- Decide if you want to be a member of a club.

- Join a few book clubs that interest you and participate in them.

- Decide if you want to host workshops, chats or book discussions.

You will do this for each book you write. You want to make sure these book clubs are current each year.

MONTHLY
- Schedule dates to visit book clubs.
- Send out letters to book clubs.
- Schedule workshops/chats or book discussions.

WEEKLY
- Visit book clubs.

DAILY
- On the day of your workshop/chat/discussion, make sure to show up on time.
- Present your workshop/chat or discuss your book.
- Answer questions and comments.

HOW TO USE FOR PROMOTION

- Have a few games to play during the discussion.
- Offer a couple prizes to those who attend.
- Send the book club a sneak peek of your next book and ask to be scheduled for another chat in the future.
- Create book discussion questions.

Online Radio

18

Online book clubs can be a fun way to introduce your books to new readers and a nice way for you to build your fan base.

Have you researched the online radio
shows that promote your genre?

ONLINE RADIO

Online radio is an excellent way to promote you and your book. Many online radio shows are in need of topics and guests. If you have a topic that fits into their needs, you could be on your way to introducing yourself to the shows' loyal listeners.

There are three forms of online radio. The first are local radio shows broadcasting online. The second are live shows broadcasting only online, consisting of an interview and callers asking questions. The last type is online radio shows that are taped and broadcasted later. They can also consist of an interview and callers asking questions.

Do an online search for online radio shows and see what you come up with; you'll be surprised how many shows are out there looking for guests. Check out your fellow writers and see what shows have featured them. Try to pick out at least ten shows to contact.

You want to find shows that fit the genre you write. I recommend listening to shows you're interested in being a guest on before contacting the hosts. It gives you a chance to hear how the show's host interacts with guests and it gives you a feel of the pace of the show.

You don't want to be on a show where the host is constantly harassing guests. You want to inform the listeners, not be on constant guard. You also don't want to come across high-strung, tongue-tied or worse...have nothing to contribute to the conversation.

HOW TO GET ON A SHOW

How can I get on a show? That's the number one question. I hear it all the time. It's not that hard, but it does take time and patience.

You found a show you like and think you'll make an excellent guest. First, check to see if the show has guidelines posted. If not, most shows will have contact information. If you have a publicist, notify them of the show and have them contact the show on your behalf.

If you don't have a publicist, send a short email introducing you and your book. Suggest a topic you feel will be of interest to their listeners. Ask if you can send an electronic press kit with an electronic copy of your book. The host or producer will contact you requesting the press kit and ask for questions pertaining to the topic. I recommend you do not send your info unless asked. You're trying to save funds, not waste them.

Send the press kit as quickly as possible and include at least ten questions about the topic and your book because sometimes hosts don't have time to read your book and having pre-prepared questions gives them an idea where to focus the interview.

YOU'VE BEEN ASKED TO BE A GUEST

Never done a radio interview? Don't worry, if you prepare beforehand, you'll sound like a pro.

Listen to the shows. See how the hosts conduct interviews. What type of questions did they ask? Do they give the guest time to answer or do they monopolize the time?

As I said before, always submit a list of questions. This is your chance to promote yourself and your book. You don't want to miss an opportunity to talk about your book. It also prepares you on what questions to expect in the interview. Most hosts do not send questions beforehand. They like to be spontaneous.

If you get lucky and the radio shows send questions, practice answering your questions. I suggest talking into a tape recorder. It lets you know how you sound. I found out I sounded like a professional Minnie Mouse after my first interview. You can't change what you sound like, however you will be prepared for how your taped voice sounds.

Practice will help you see if you do a lot of hemming and hawing (i.e., uhm, uh, hmm) and make weird sounds when you talk. This is natural, but if you practice, you can learn to eliminate them.

BEFORE THE INTERVIEW

• Have your notes in front of you.

• Have a glass of water for when your mouth is dry.

DURING THE INTERVIEW

Take your time and listen to the host. This will calm your nerves. I always say a prayer before an interview. This usually calms me.

Try to answer the question the best you can. If you don't know, say so and that you'll get back to them with the answer.

Always give the title of your book, where it can be purchased, your website and email.

If you want to see who is listening, offer a freebie to the listeners. You always want to build on your reader base. Have them sign up for your mailing list to receive it. Thank the host while on the interview.

AFTER THE INTERVIEW

Send a thank you note to the host for the interview and let them know you are always available for future interviews. Even offer a few topics, if you have them.

Post the interview link on your site the day of the interview. Send out the information to your mailing lists, forums and social media.

Listen to the interview and take notes on how you did. What can you do to improve your interviews for future use?

Now you're a pro at online radio interviews and ready for the next one.

MY EXPERIENCE

I got into online radio by accident. It was before blog talk radio came into existence. MYBOOKRADIO was an online radio show network. I visited the site and loved the concept of all-book radio shows. I wrote the owner and told her I would love to see some shows that featured African American writers. She suggested I do my own show. Shades Radio was born. It was a weekly show where I featured a guest and talked about books.

I had to learn how to set up a radio show, break for commercials and tape my interview since the broadcast was taped and not live. It was a fun experience and I learned a lot about doing live interviews. The show lasted a year.

ACTION PLAN

LaShaunda's Tip

I used to host my own radio show. It was a weekly show. You can create your own radio show. Interview guests, talk about a topic that's important to you. This is a good way to reach new readers.

Getting Started

Here are a few radio shows to get you started:
* http://www.blogtalkradio.com/themathellgivenshow
* http://www.blogtalkradio.com/ashea-goldson#
* http://www.blogtalkradio.com/black-author-network
* http://www.blogtalkradio.com/readyoulater

There are many online radio shows now. This is why the search engine is your friend. You can find a radio show for every genre. Find ten shows and listen to them. If it's a good fit for you, send an introduction letter.

What you need to know:

- Name of host.

    - Contact's email address.

    - When and how they want to be contacted.

    - What type of topics are they looking for (guidelines)?

    - Who are their readers?

    - What topics would you like to pitch?

- Write your introduction letter.

Schedule Your Calendar

- Pick a day and set an actual time you can sit down to research online radio shows that promote your genre.

- Keep a log of whom you sent letters to and when you sent them, and include who accepted them and who rejected them.

- Schedule a date to write introduction letters.

- Schedule interview dates.

- Schedule dates for promotion.

- Schedule time on your calendar for the next lesson—Online Magazines.

Promotion Plan
YEARLY

- Research online radio shows that feature your genre. Select five to ten shows to contact.

MONTHLY

- Listen to shows you selected. See if they are where you want to promote your book.

- Choose shows that you'd feel comfortable as a guest.

- Create your introduction letter and send out to the shows.

- Schedule interview dates.

- Send content needed for the interview.

WEEKLY

- Promote the interview on your site/newsletter and social media.

HOW TO USE FOR PROMOTION

- Host a launch party.

- Be a guest on a panel.

- Be a featured author.

- Talk about the theme of your book.

- Talk about current events.

Online Magazines

*Have you researched online magazines that
promote your genre?*

What I like about being online is there is something for everyone.
For instance, if you write romance, you probably will find a few
sites that promote romance, or if you write mystery, you'll find
the mystery sites.

That can also be said for online magazines. When I started
SORMAG, there weren't many online magazines. Now there are
many online magazines that promote books and writers.

MY EXPERIENCE

I created SORMAG because there wasn't an online magazine
that catered to the African American reader or writer of romance.
I loved reading romance, contemporary and historical. I wanted
to help promote these book and their writers.

For most of the interviews I've conducted for the magazine,
I contacted the authors. However, I really like to be contacted
by an author who has a promotion plan. They have researched
the magazine or have been following the magazine for years.

They approach me by sending an email, telling me who they are, introducing their book, why they think the readers would like to hear about them and how to contact them.

I will immediately contact them. They've made my job easy. Every now and then, I will receive a letter from a writer who says "check out my site." No title, no name, just a link. Why make my life hard? Guess who doesn't get an interview.

RESEARCH

As with any magazine, most work with a schedule. I recommend that you do your research well before approaching them.

Find the magazines that promote your genre, as well as other genres. For example, SORMAG started as a romance magazine, but over the years, we moved to promoting all literature, so you might find a romance or a mystery or even a history book featured.

Do not count out the magazine if they promote one genre; your book might still interest their audience. This is where articles come in. If their audience is the readers you are looking for, you can write an article for them and still get a chance to promote your book in your bio.

- Read and adhere to their submission guidelines.
- How do they want you to introduce yourself?
- Do they want you to send a book for review?
- Do they offer guest spots or articles?
- Do they offer free promotion or only paid promotion?
- Look at their paid promotion.
- Is it something that fits into your budget?

CREATE A LIST

Create a list with ten magazines to get you started. You can always add to your list once you get the hang of approaching magazines.

Start with the free promotion. Set up your interviews or promotions by sending your letter of introduction. Offer to be interviewed, do a guest post or write an article.

Do not expect to get a promotion the month you contact them. If your book is coming out, try to schedule your interview three to six months in advance. Remember most magazines are on a schedule of three to six months in advance. Check their guidelines for submissions.

INTERVIEWS

Read over the interview. Gather information they need for the interview. Answer the questions, try to refrain from one-word answers. You want an interesting interview, so pretend you're having a conversation and let the words flow. Make sure you return the interview on time.

Please meet the magazine's deadlines. There's nothing like having an interview scheduled and the author doesn't submit the information for the interview. Don't have the magazine chasing you down. Always be professional and submit your interview or article on time.

Include a picture of yourself and your book. This helps the editor not have to go in search of this information.

Ask when your interview/article will go live. Send the link out to your friends, family and fans. Stop by the site/blog to see if the interview/article is live. Leave a comment or answer questions, if there are any.

FOLLOW UP

Send a thank you note to the magazine for featuring you. Let them know you stopped by and read the interview and offer your services for future issues.

PROMOTING

Promoting with an online magazine can be fun and interactive. Some offer chats and other ways to interact with their readers. Take time to get to know the magazines. Build a relationship with them. Online magazines can help you build your writing career.

Don't expect to continue to receive freebies when you're not supporting them. Online magazines are loyal to those who are loyal to them. With your next book, remember to support the magazine if it offers paid promotion. Schedule them into your budget. Remember, if you don't support them, they can't support you. This is a business. You need each other to stay in business.

YOU'VE BEEN ASKED FOR AN INTERVIEW, NOW WHAT?

Here are a few tips to help you have a great interview.

1.   Complete the interview.

A lot of authors miss their opportunity for an interview because they don't complete the interview.

2. Copy and paste the interview.

   Most blogs/sites copy and paste the interview to their posts. It's a lot easier for them if you copy and paste the interview with the questions and answers intact. Don't make extra work for them by just sending them the answers and no questions. You don't want them trying to figure out which answer goes with which question.

3. Include a picture.

   Readers like to see what the author looks like. If you don't have pictures, invest in you and get professional pictures taken.

4. Include an email or contact information.

   Readers like sending emails or letters to their favorite author. They can't do this if you don't have a way to contact you. Include a link to your website, invite the reader to stop by and join your mailing list.

5. Be on time.

   Make sure your completed interview reaches the site/ blog in time for them to post on the date scheduled.

6. Visit the site/blog featuring your interview.

   Take time to visit the site/blog to see what the interview looks like. Check to see everything you sent is featured. The links are correct, no typos. Errors can be made, however if you don't say anything the site/blog owner will never know.

If it's a blog, leave a comment for the readers. Blog visitors like to see that the featured author took time to say hello. Make time to answer a few questions.

7. Offer an autographed book or prize for a lucky winner.

   Contests are good ways to draw readers, which adds new people to your mailing list.

8. Send out an announcement to your mailing list, newsletter and social media.

   Let your readers know about your interview. This will introduce them to the site/blog and they will learn a little more about you, their favorite author.

9. Include a link on your site.

   This is a nice way to thank the person interviewing you. Links are forever and whenever someone reads the post, they can click on the interview and visit a new site.

10. Send a thank you note/email.

    This will let the site/blog/magazine owner know you appreciate the interview and that you saw the interview. You can also let them know you're available for future interviews.

An interview is a fun way to promote your book. Take time to schedule one or two interviews a month.

You want to make the magazine editor's life easier. Do your homework, approach them right and receive an interview.

CTION PLAN

LaShaunda's Tip
Magazines are always looking for fresh content. You can be the writer they need. Pitch a few articles or become a columnist.

Getting Started
What you need to know for online magazine:

* Name of host.
  * Contact's name and email address.
  * When and how they want to be contacted.
  * What type of topics are they looking for (guidelines)?
  * Who are their readers?
  * What topics would you like to pitch?
* Write your introduction letter.

Here are a few online magazines to get you started:
* http://sormag.com
* http://www.blackpearlsmagazine.com/
* http://www.indtale.com
* http://www.southernwritersmagazine.com/
* http://www.christianfictiononlinemagazine.com/

Schedule Your Calendar

- Pick a day and set an actual time you can sit down to research online magazines that promote your genre.

- Keep a log of whom you sent letters to and when you sent them, and include who accepted them and who rejected them.

- Schedule a date to write pitch letters.

- Schedule a date to write introduction letters.

- Schedule time on your calendar for the next lesson—Online Chats.

Promotion Plan
YEARLY

- Research online magazines that feature your genre, and select five to ten to contact.

MONTHLY

- Visit the magazines you selected, and see if you want to promote your book with them.

- Choose those you'd feel comfortable being featured in.

- Create your introduction letter and send out to the magazines.

- Schedule interview dates.

- Send the magazines content they need for the interview—and in a timely manner.

WEEKLY

- Promote the interview on your site/newsletter and social media.

HOW TO USE ONLINE
MAGAZINES FOR PROMOTION

- Have your book featured as the Book Of The Day/Week/ Month.
- Be a featured author in the magazine.
- Create an ad to be featured in the magazine.
- Be a guest columnist for the magazine.
- Write an article for the magazine.

Online Chats

Chats are another way to communicate with your readers. You can host monthly chats and see your readership build. My favorite historical romance author, Beverly Jenkins, hosts monthly chats with her fans. It's a real treat to ask about the characters that you've grown to love.

You can even use the chat room to feature other authors you know. Readers love chatting with authors.

You can chat many ways online. Skype, Google+ Hangout, and Twitter chats are fast-paced forum chats.

CHAT ROOMS

Chat rooms can be hosted on a site using chat room software. For example, a Twitter chat can be hosted in a Twitter Chat room. Readers log in to the chat and type comments and questions that you would answer.

PHONE CHATS

Phone chats are another way to host live chats. You can set up a telephone chat using a free service, such as freeconference. com. Do a search for conference call services.

You can do so many things with phone chats. You can host phone chats, or be a participant in someone else's. I use phone chats for author interviews that become podcasts, to host online conferences, for book discussions, and webinars, tele-summits or workshops.

FACE-TO-FACE CHATS

Face-to-face is the new way to chat. You can utilize a few systems to have face-to-face chats with your readers using your laptop or cell phone. Skype or Google Hangouts are tools you can use for face-to-face. The readers can see you and you can see them. This works great for book clubs or events you can't attend.

WHAT TO CHAT ABOUT?

Upcoming releases, writing techniques, favorite characters and great loves scenes, etc. Maybe your book's theme is about something you think your readers would be interested in discussing. The chat room could be used for this discussion.

TIPS FOR A SUCCESSFUL CHAT

- Do prepare in advance.
- Practice answering questions.
- Promote it a week or two before on your newsletter, site, and social media, listing chat time, day and location.
- The day of the chat, send a reminder.
- Use the bathroom before the chat.
- Have a glass of water in front of you. Don't include ice because ice jingles during a live chat.

- Try not to drink too much before and during the chat.

- Always log into a chat at least five minutes earlier. Chat rooms tend to have connection issues. (Some chat rooms require software download for use. You want to give yourself plenty of time to sign in.) You don't want to miss the chat because you waited too late to sign on.

- Have a brief bio, mention your site and a little about the topic you plan to discuss.

- Answer questions personally. Attendees like to feel you're talking to them.

- Be aware that some chat rooms do not allow cut and paste, so type fast.

- Make sure you reply to all questions. Scroll through the chat.

- Be prepared for being booted out of the chat room.

- Offer giveaways (I like to give gifts to the first and the last to attend the chat).

- Give a sample chapter of upcoming release to those who email you after the chat. (Great database builder.)

- It doesn't matter how many people attend the chat. (Some of the best chats have been with five or less people. I find them more personal.)

- If the transcript is posted afterwards, this is an excellent way for more promotion, especially for those who missed the chat.

- Always send a thank you note to the chat host. Check with them later to schedule another chat.

HOSTING A CHAT

Hosting a chat is a great way for self-promotion on the net. You get a chance to meet your readers and discuss your book.

You've never hosted a chat?

It's not that hard. Once you survive the first one, you'll be eager to do more. If you design your website right, your site can have its own chat room. If not, you can use a free one; do a search to find one that is compatible with your site.

Just be warned—with free comes advertisement that you have no control over. Also, your guests will have to sign up to use them.

Before you host a chat, I recommend you play with the chat room you're going to use. You want to get a feel for the chat room. You don't want to find out the day of the chat that you don't know how it works, or that you can't even get into the software.

Chatting is a fun way to get to know your readers. It's a great way to share your writing wisdom and make new fans. Start scheduling those chats.

RULES

Always have rules for a chat even if it's open. Chatters like to follow some type of protocol.

- Is this chat protocol or open?
- No chatting while the guest is chatting.
- How should the chatter send in his question?
- No flaming (disrespect, cursing, etc.) of anyone in the chat, including the speaker.

START THE CHAT

- Open the chat for chatting.

- Welcome the chatters.

- Explain the protocol for the chat. Will it be open or a question/answer chat?

- Give the rules of the chat.

- Introduce yourself and talk a little about your book. If you have a topic for the chat, talk about that. Then open it up for questions.

- The first chatter to type the question mark (?) is your first question.

- Maintain a list of whose next for questions.

- Make sure everyone who is participating gets his or her questions asked.

- If no one is asking questions, you can always start up a topic. You never want a blank screen. Always have extra topics on hand. This is a chance to ask your own questions.

END THE CHAT

- Inform the chatters when the session is over.

- Thank everyone for coming to the chat.

- Offer a copy of an excerpt if they send you their email address (build up your database).

- Giveaway for attendees (autographed books or small prizes).

- If you're making a transcript, let them know how to get a copy or see the final result.

THE LANGUAGE OF CHATS

Open chat—everyone chats freely, no rules. Sometimes these types of chats are hard to follow for new chatters, because everyone is chatting at the same time.

Protocol—is when you control the chat room. In protocol, you tell the chatters how the chat will be handled. This is not an open chat where everyone talks at one time. The chatters have to type the question mark (?) sign if they have a question. It makes the chat go without complications and everyone gets their questions asked.

Here are some chat room lingoes:

!	"I have a comment"
$0.02	Throwing in your two cents' worth
<g>	Grin
<grin>	Indicates the speaker is grinning
<smile>	Indicates the one writing the message is smiling
?	I have a question
A-OLs	Administrators On-Line—Administrators who police on-line services
B4N	Bye For Now
BBIAB	Be Back In A Bit
BBIAF	Be Back In A Few (minutes)
BBL	Be Back Later
BRB	Be Right Back
GA	Go Ahead
IMHO	In My Humble Opinion

IMNSHO	In My Not So Humble Opinion
IMO	In My Opinion
JMO	Just My Opinion
LLTA	Lots and Lots of Thunderous (or Thundering) Applause
LMAO	Laughing My Ass Off
LMHO	Laughing My Head Off
LOL	Laughing Out Loud
LSHMBA	Laughing So Hard My Belly Aches
LSHMBH	Laughing So Hard My Belly Hurts
LTHTT	Laughing Too Hard To Type
LY	Love You
OTFL	On the Floor Laughing
ROFL	Rolling On Floor Laughing
SWIM	See What I Mean?
THX	Thanks
TIA	Thanks In Advance
TRDMC	Tears Running Down My Cheeks
WB	Welcome Back
WTG	Way To Go!
XOXOXO	Kisses and hugs
:)	Happy
: ( )	Loud Mouth
:-O	Surprise
:(or :-(	Frown
;) or ;-)	Wink
:P or :-P	Sticking tongue out (sometimes done playfully among friends)
:-/	Confused of perplexed
:-0	Shocked

TYPING IN ALL CAPS is considered SCREAMING and is generally frowned upon.

MY EXPERIENCE

I love chats. They are a fun way to interact with readers. I used to host a monthly chat with the forum I hosted and with SORMAG. I've participated in chat rooms with crazy software that had a habit of kicking you out of the room. Many chat rooms have improved over the years.

I've chatted using Twitter Chat; it's very fast and you have to keep up with the posts because they move quickly.

My favorite chats are phone chats because I like talking more than typing. Phone chats are more intimate and you can hear the author's voice.

I do recommend if you are doing phone chats to use a landline because the sound is better, which makes for a better recording if the call is recorded.

Cell phones tend to warble their sound and often drop in the middle of the call. The last thing you want on a chat is the listeners not to hear you or for the call to drop.

CTION PLAN

LaShaunda's Tip

Google+ Hangout Air is the new chat live, face-to-face chat. Check out a few hangouts to get a feel of participating in a live chat.

Getting Started

- You can create your own chats with your readers. Do something monthly or quarterly.

- Find sites, groups or book clubs that host chats.

- Choose the ones that you'd feel comfortable being a part of.

- Create your introduction letter and send out.

- Schedule dates for the chats.

- Send content if they need it.

- Schedule your own chats.

Schedule Your Calendar

- Schedule dates to request invites for chats.
- Schedule dates for chats.
- Schedule dates to send thank you notes for chats.
- Schedule date for next lesson—Online Events.

Promotion Plan
YEARLY

- Research other places you can have chats (book clubs, groups, sites etc.).
- Decide if you will host your own chats.

MONTHLY

- Visit the places you selected. Sit in on one of their chats to see if it's something you want to do.

WEEKLY

- Promote the chats on your site/newsletter and social media.

HOW TO USE CHATS FOR PROMOTION

- Host a monthly reader's chat
- Host a book discussion chat
- Host a Q&A chat
- Participate in Google + Hangouts
- Host a chat with other writers in your genre

Online Events 21

One of my favorite places to find new readers is an online event, which can be teleseminars, online conferences, workshops, or webinars.

These events are great ways to promote you and your book. You can offer freebies, even if you don't think you have anything to offer, or volunteer to host a workshop. Attend different events to get your name out there. When the opportunity arises, talk about yourself and your book and invite those attendees to your site.

The best part about an online event is if you can't find any to attend, you can create your own, which, is what I did. It was a great time and I didn't have to leave my home. It took place on my computer screen. You can do the same thing. I'd say start small and work your way up to a big event.

Online launch parties are another fun way to introduce your new book. You can have a live event just like a real launch party only everything is happening online.

Be creative and create your own events to draw new readers to you.

MY EXPERIENCE

I created my own online event with the SORMAG Online Conference. It was a lot of work, but worth the networking and database building. I've also hosted and taught workshops and attended countless webinars and teleseminars online. I highly recommend attending at least two to three online events a year.

CTION PLAN

LaShaunda's Tip
I created the SORMAG Online Conference because I wanted to attend a writing conference, but I didn't have the funds or the vacation time. I created a seven-day, online conference that featured writers, agents, editors and readers. You can do the same and create an event that caters to your genre.

Getting Started
Here are a few questions to ask about online events:
• Have you attended any online events before?
• Do you like presenting workshops online?
• Do you have topics to discuss or information to share?
• How many events would you like to do for the year?
• Would you like to host your own event?
• What type of event will you host?
• Who will be a part of the event?
• What are the dates of the event?

- What marketing products do you need for the event?
- Do you need a team for your event?

Schedule Your Calendar

- Pick a day and set an actual time you can sit down to research online events that promote your genre.
- Schedule a date to write introduction letters.
- Schedule dates for your own events.
- Schedule time on your calendar for the next lesson— Podcasts/Videos.

Promotion Plan
YEARLY
- Research online events that feature your genre, and select five to ten to contact.
- Decide if you will host your own online events.

MONTHLY
- Visit the events you selected. See if they are where you want to promote your book.
- Choose the events you feel comfortable participating in.
- Create your introduction letter and send out to the events.
- Schedule dates for the events.
- Send needed content to the events.
- Schedule your event dates.

WEEKLY
- Promote the events on your site/newsletter and social media.

WAYS TO USE ONLINE EVENTS
FOR PROMOTION

- Host a workshop
- Offer giveaway prizes
- Be a sponsor
- Volunteer to moderate a class
- Host a book discussion
- Launch party
- Blog hops

Podcasts/Videos

This next lesson, I will admit to being a newbie. Over the last few years, I've been learning about podcasts and using video as a promotional tool.

I enjoy learning from podcasts and videos so I can see how they can be great as a way to meet new readers.

You can create your own promotional podcasts or videos and post them on your site, YouTube, in your newsletters or social media.

PODCASTS

Podcasts are audios that come in the form of MP3 files. They can be short audios or one to two hours long. It all depends on the subject of the podcasts.

Podcasts can be:
- Author interviews
- Writing workshop (craft, business, etc.)
- Book excerpts

- Writing advice
- Live or prerecorded

Last year I decided to try my hand at podcasts. I created: SORMAG's Writer's Café and See Ya On The Net Podcasts—Tips for promoting online, and I'm learning something new with each podcast. They are a fun way to promote. You choose what topics you want to talk about, and you can do them by yourself or invite guests. If you don't want to produce your own podcasts, you can be a guest on someone else's.

PRODUCING YOUR PODCAST

Spreaker.com and soundcloud.com are two places you can use to produce your podcast. They are free sites. Do your research and find places that can help you produce podcasts and host them.

VIDEOS

Now that everyone has a smartphone, making videos have become easy. Most smartphones come with a recorder or you can download one. Or, if you have the budget you can get video equipment to use for your videos.

Like podcasts, videos can be used to do interviews, workshops or create book trailers. If the camera doesn't intimidate you, you can create a weekly vlog (video blog) and talk to your readers.

I haven't stepped in front of the camera to film my own videos, however I have been taped for someone else's videos. I will admit it can be a little intimidating, but if you have a good host, they can put you at ease.

If you're taping your own, you will get more comfortable in front of the camera with each episode you tape.

Don't let fear stop you from trying something new. I always say try it once. If you don't like it, move on to something new.

As for videos, YouTube is the place to be when it comes to videos. I suggest you stop by and spend a few hours watching videos. This will help you determine if video is something you want to do.

Since I don't have much experience in video, I recommend LaShanda Henry. Check out her videos on YouTube. She will take you step by step on how to create your own videos.

MY EXPERIENCE

I told you about Shades Radio. I enjoyed the experience of doing live interviews. Before my podcast, I did a lot of listening to podcasts. I enjoyed the format of a live interview or offering advice of some type.

I'm working on another podcast to debut next year: LaShaunda's Business Tips—Lessons I've Learned About Being An Entrepreneur.

What I love about podcasting is that there is a podcast for every niche. Do your research and you can find the perfect podcast for you.

For videos, I like watching how-to videos. There are videos for different genres. For example, I watch natural hair videos, videos on marketing, videos on writing and videos on business. I like being able to find a subject and finding a video that will help me. You could be the writer creating those videos or podcasts.

CTION PLAN

LaShaunda's Tip
Listen to other podcasts and videos to get a feel of how they work. Is this something you would like to do?

Getting Started
* Here are few questions to ask:.
    * Do you like talking or talking in front of a camera?
    * Do you have topics or information to share?
    * How many podcasts or videos would you like do for the year?
    * Where will you host your podcast/video?
    * What will your podcast/video be about?
    * How long will the podcast/video be?
    * How often will the podcast/video be broadcasted?
    * Will it be live or taped?
    * Where will you post the podcast/video?
* Research different podcasts hosts and video hosts.
* Create your profiles or channels.
* Create a few practice podcasts/videos.
* Listen to some podcasts/videos to get a feel of them.

Schedule Your Calendar
* Pick a day and set an actual time you can sit down to research podcasts and videos and where to host them.

- Schedule a date to write your podcast scripts or video scripts.

- Schedule dates to promote your podcasts/videos.

- Schedule dates to load podcasts or videos to hosting sites and websites.

- Schedule time on your calendar for the next lesson— Reviews/Online Bookstores.

Promotion Plan
YEARLY

- Decide if you will create podcasts/videos?

- How often will you produce them?

- Research places to host your podcast/videos.

- Research how you will create them.

MONTHLY

- Decide on the topics for the year.

- How many to create each month?

- Will you have guests?

- Create a letter to invite guests?

- Decide on dates to create podcast/video.

- Decide on dates for podcast/video to go live.

- Schedule your event dates.

WEEKLY

- Promote podcast/video on your site/newsletter and social media.

WAYS TO USE PODCASTS/VIDEOS
FOR PROMOTION

- Create a workshop
- Create tutorial
- Interview your favorite author
- Talk about how you started writing
- Review a book

Reviews And Online Book Stores

23

REVIEW SITES, BOOK BLOGS OR BOOK CLUBS

If you are working with a publisher, make sure you have a list from your publisher of the reviewers they sent your book to, because you don't want to send your book to the same reviewers.

If you are self-publishing, research online to find the sites that offer reviews for the genre you write.

Many sites feature reviews and love featuring new writers. Check their review guidelines. Some might request the book be sent before you contact, while other want you to contact them prior to sending the book. Make sure you know their guidelines and what they review. Sending out reviews is costly; you want to send your books to the reviewers who will read your book.

REVIEWS FROM READERS

There's nothing wrong with asking your readers to post a review on an online bookstore. Some will take the time to post an honest review.

Ask them to review the book when you autograph it, when they win a copy, or when they contact you to tell you how much they love it. Ask for reviews on your social media. You can't get reviews if you don't ask for them.

Many readers are intimidated by posting reviews to online bookstores or maybe they don't have an account with the site and they don't want to create one. In this case, ask them to send you the review.

The reader might feel comfortable sending you the review versus posting the review. Think about how writers received reviews before social media and online sites. Readers used to write letters to their favorite authors. If you're having trouble having your readers post reviews, this a good suggestion for getting reviews.

You can still use these reviews on your site. Create a page on your site that features these reviews. You can include this link in your promotions.

AFTER YOU RECEIVE THE REVIEW

When the reviewer or reader sends you a review, post it on your site, newsletter, mailing list and social media. You can pull quotes and feature them in your marketing material.

Make sure to send a thank you note.

If the review isn't what you expect, don't complain to the reviewer. Keep opinions to yourself. You don't want to ruin a relationship because you received a lower rating. Just because you love your book doesn't mean everyone else will. It comes with the territory. Suck it up and move on to the next review.

ONLINE BOOKSTORES

Research and find the bookstores that feature your genre. See if they offer author pages. Create your pages on each site. Include information about you, links to your site and social media.

Check to see if they feature reviews. Do you have any reviews listed? If not, ask your readers to post reviews on the site.

MY EXPERIENCE

With SORMAG, we offer reviews. I recommend reading the guidelines for where you plan to send review requests. You can't imagine how many books I used to receive that weren't geared toward SORMAG readers. I didn't return books, so the author spent money on postage and didn't receive a review. Do your research, save yourself some money and get the reviews you want.

CTION PLAN

LaShaunda's Tip
Reviews are the word of mouth that works. Try to get as many as you can. Create an incentive for your readers to write a review. Also, save on postage and find sites that accept PDFs or ecopies.

Getting Started
- Find review sites—read the guidelines
- Package your ARC (advance reading copy) for mailing
- Submit to sites

Schedule Your Calendar
- Schedule dates to research review sites and reviews.
- Schedule dates to set up author pages on online bookstores.
- Schedule time on your calendar for the next lesson— Scheduled Promotion.

Promotion Plan
YEARLY
- Research review sites, and pick twelve.

MONTHLY
- Submit your book for review.

WEEKLY
- Check for reviews.
- Send thank you notes/letters

WAYS TO USE REVIEWS AND ONLINE BOOK STORES FOR PROMOTION

- Quotes for reviews
- Feature reviews in newsletter
- Promote on website

Schedule Promotion

Have you created a schedule for your online promotion?
Have you scheduled your free promotion?
Have you scheduled your paid promotion?

FREE PROMOTION

Most writers have a small budget to work with, so the first thing you want to do is find all the free sites to promote your books. You want to work with them first and choose the sites that introduce you to the most new readers for the place you spend your budget.

Because free promotion is not easy to come by, you have to do your research. Be prepared with what is needed of you; submit it in a timely manner so you don't mess up someone's schedule.

PAID PROMOTION

One of the things I learned when I sold Mary Kay Cosmetics is that you have to spend money to make money. This is so true when it comes to promoting your books. You want to reach as many readers as you can, which means sometimes you have to pay for promotion.

When you start your research, you will find that most magazines/sites/blogs offer free and paid promotion. Check out their advertising page. Look at the promotions that fit your budget. Sometimes magazines will work with you and your budget. ASK! All they can say is *no*.

Select the promotion that fits your budget and send them the information they need to create the promotion.

Ask for a date it will go live and make sure you receive a copy of the promotion or know where it is located.

Send the link to your friends, family and fans.

Let the magazine/site/blog know you saw the ad and if you liked or didn't like it.

Refer your friends if the magazine/site/blog did a good promotion.

Remember with any promotion, paid or free, there is no guarantee of a sale. The objective of promotion is to introduce your book to new readers. Keeping your name in front of the readers is your goal.

RETURN ON INVESTMENT (ROI)

What would you like your ad to do for you?

- Sell Books?
- Introduce you to new readers?
- Get readers to sign up for your mailing list/newsletter?

This will be your call to action when you create your ad space.

Most writers buy ad space, but don't think about a call toaction, which means they don't have any idea if they received return on their investment (ROI). How do you know if the ad is working for you?

You have to decide what you want the ad to do for you. I'm sure you would like all three, but you want to make the reader make a decision quickly. So, which decision is the question you need to know.

Sell Books
You want to make sure you include a link to purchase your book. Send the reader to the store on your website or send them to an online bookstore. You want them to buy the book NOW.

Introduce you to new readers.
You want to make sure you include a link to your social media and website. Send the reader to where they can connect with you.

Get readers to sign up for your mailing list/newsletter.
You want to include a link to your mailing list or newsletter form. Send the reader to your site so they can fill out the form and become a part of your community.

Schedule the date for promotion. Make sure to send all the information the magazine/site needs to promote your ad.

On the date of the promotion, check the magazine/site. Some magazines/sites will send you a link for the promotion, if they don't, make sure to check the ad is what you paid for.

Promote the link on your social media, newsletter and sites. You want the biggest bang for your promotional dollars. Sharing the information is how you do it.

MY EXPERIENCE

Scheduling promotion has always been helpful for me. It's how I run SORMAG. I schedule free promotion and paid promotion. I'm able to track whom I'm featuring on SORMAG's Blog or in the digital magazine for the year.

I also schedule promotion for SORMAG with other sites and through social media. I'm always promoting in some form or fashion.

I'm currently scheduling my own promotions. I'm doing more online radio interviews and podcasts.

I find scheduling my promotion keeps me and SORMAG in front of the readers at all times.

ONLINE PROMOTION—FREE

Sites for Free Promotion	Promotion Dates
1.	
2.	
3.	
4.	
5.	
6.	
7.	
8.	
9.	
10.	
11.	
12.	
13.	

ONLINE PROMOTION—PAID PROMOTION

BUDGET $_____

Site to Advertise With	Ad Rate
1.	
2.	
3.	
4.	
5.	
6.	
7.	
8.	
9.	
10.	
11.	
12.	
13.	
14.	
15.	
16.	
17.	
18.	
19.	
20.	
TOTAL FOR ADS:	$
BUDGET SPENT	$

CTION PLAN

LaShaunda's Tip
SORMAG is a great place to promote your book for free and for paid advertisement. We feature author interviews, books of the day, articles, short stories, blog tours and podcasts. We cater to the multi-cultural reader and writer. We offer a digital magazine and online blog. However, we are not the only online magazine out there.

Getting Started
- Research the sites, blogsand magazines that cater to your genre.
- Read over their guidelines for promotion.
- Send the letter of introduction, and offer your services for an interview, article, etc.
- Visit each site on the day of the promotion. Answer questions if there are any.
- Send a thank you note after the promotion.

Schedule Your Calendar
- Schedule dates to research free and paid promotion sites.
- Schedule dates for free and paid promotion.
- Schedule dates for promoting promotions.
- Schedule date for next lesson—Using Your Online Promotion Plan.

Promotion Plan
YEARLY
- Research places to promote your book.
- Decide your budget.

MONTHLY
- Create letters of introduction.
- Decide on dates for free promotions.
- Decide dates for paid promotions.

WEEKLY
- Promote promotions on your site/newsletter and social media.

HOW TO USE FOR PROMOTION

- Advertising your new release
- Featured author on a site
- Advertise your upcoming workshop
- Book spotlight on a site
- Blog tours

25
Your Online Promotion Plan

GETTING STARTED

Pick one day of the week to sit down and create your online promotion plan.

Look at the hours you would like to designate for your promotion time, and schedule time throughout the month to get in your promotion time.

There are twelve months in the year, and I suggest you have something to do for your marketing for each month.

Get your calendar out and let's get down to scheduling dates.

Each action plan will help you create a schedule that works for you.

Start with free promotion. How many sites/blogs/magazines fit into your budget?

Which sites have the readers you're looking for?

Then move on to the paid promotion. Your budget will determine how much you will spend.

Create a list of whom you would like to advertise with from sites you researched earlier.

Check out the sites that fit in your budget. Make sure you check their guidelines for submitting your advertising information. You don't want to wait until the last minute and miss their deadlines.

Make sure they have all the information needed to create the advertisement. You don't want them hunting you down for information, and again you miss the deadline.

SAMPLE THREE-MONTH ONLINE PROMOTION PLAN

January
- Introduce myself to ten book bloggers
- Introduce myself to ten radio hosts
- Set up Blog
- Place a Coming Soon ad on SORMAG
- Comment on Facebook and Twitter twice a day
- Write a blog post twice a week
- Send out monthly newsletter
- Update my email signature

February
- Set up a ten-site blog tour
- Answer blog tour interviews
- Write blog entries for the month
- Network more on Facebook
- Comment on Facebook and Twitter twice a day
- Update website
- Send out monthly newsletter
- Update My email signature

March
- Set up five book signings
- Set up blog entries for month
- Comment on Facebook and Twitter twice a day
- Update website
- Send out monthly newsletter
- Update my email signature

ONLINE PROMOTION PLAN

JANUARY
- _____
- _____
- _____
- _____
- _____

FEBRUARY
- _____
- _____
- _____
- _____
- _____

MARCH
- _____
- _____
- _____
- _____
- _____

HOW DO YOU KNOW IF YOUR PROMOTION IS WORKING?

In the paid promotion section, I mentioned three ways you know ads are working. You can use those and a few more to see if your promotion is working.

1. Are you selling books?

   Your royalty checks or your business bank account should reflect books sold. The object of being a writer is to sell your books. If you are not selling books, you definitely are doing something wrong and you need to sit down and reevaluate what you're doing and try to improve on it.

   Are your reviews saying positive or negative things about your writing? Maybe you need to look at your writing.

   Look at your promotions. How did each promotion do? Did you see a jump in sales for each promotion?

2. Did you meet new readers?

   You should be trying to meet new readers daily. You can do this by blogging, visiting blogs, forums, groups and social media.

   You should see an increase in your followers on your blogs and social media.

3. Have you received more reviews?

   Have you noticed more reviews on sites and online bookstores?

4. Does your mailing list or newsletter have new members since you started promoting?

5. Has your podcasts/videos been downloaded or listened to more?

6. Are you being invited to be a guest on a group, list or forum?

7. Are you being invited to be a guest blogger, article writer or be interviewed on magazines, sites?

8. Are you being asked to be a guest author by online book clubs?

9. Are you being invited to be a guest on radio shows, podcasts or hangouts?

10. Is your social media platform growing?

Closing

If you are answering "no" to the previous questions, you have a problem with your promotion. However, if you're answering "yes," as I hope you will, this book is helping you improve your promotion and has done its job.

If you are reading this page, I'm clapping for you because that means you have worked your way through the book. I hope you have done all your research and you've created a plan that works for you and your time.

Please remember this isn't a one-day plan. If you work your plan right, you should be doing something to promote your book every day. A few minutes a day and you will get your book in front of new readers.

You should also see a change in your sales, in your followers and in your mailing list.

HOW TO GET THE MOST OUT OF YOUR PROMOTION

Promotion is a good way to:
- Introduce you to readers.

- Recommend your books to readers.

- Remind readers your book is on the shelf.
- Nudge readers to think about purchasing your book.

I recommend you always have a call to action for your promotion:

1. **Buy Me Now Link**—For the reader who just might want to click now.
2. **Website Link**—Invite the reader over to your site.
3. **Join My Mailing List**—Include a link for them to join.
4. **Freebie**—Offer a freebie (excerpt, short story).

Your goal is to bring that reader to your community. You want to make those readers a part of your community by having them join your mailing list. They might not be ready to buy, but if they sign up for your mailing list that means they are interested, so you want to make sure you can turn that interest into a purchase.

Remember promotion is all about building relationships. You can't do that if you don't have a way to get in touch with them. The mailing list is what keeps you in touch. Building your mailing list means you're building relationships.

Promotion is a never-ending story. I'm always shocked to hear authors say that they don't have time to promote their books. To stay in this business you have to make time to promote if you want to see your readership grow.

Create a new plan for each book you release. If something doesn't work for you, scratch it off and move to the next thing on your list. Do what works for you and have fun.

Remember that creating an online promotion plan is a good way to keep you on track and help you reach new readers, daily.

WORKSHEETS

ONLINE PROMOTION PLAN
RESEARCH EXAMPLE BY HOURS

Promotions	Hours (10/wk)	Promotions To Do	Day To Promote	Hours Completed
Email Signature				
Database	1	Bounced Emails	Friday	2
Website/ Blog	2	Update For New Book	Thursday	1
Social Media	2	Interact With Fans	Daily	3
Sites/Blogs	1	Visit 2 Sites	Daily	1
Blog Tour				
Articles	1	Write An Article	Tuesday	2
Forums				
Online Book Clubs	1	Find 5 Book Clubs	Wednesday	
Online Radio	1	Find 2 Radio Shows	Monday	
Online Magazines	1	Complete Interview	Friday	2
TOTAL	**10**			**11**

ONLINE PROMOTION PLAN
RESEARCH SCHEDULE BY HOURS

Promotions	Hours	Research To Do	Research Days	Hours Completed
Email Signature				
Database				
Website/ Blog				
Social Media				
Sites/Blogs				
Newsletter				
Blog Tours				
Articles				
Groups				
Forums				
Book Club				
Radio				
Magazines				
Podcasts				
Events				

ONLINE PROMOTION PLAN
PROMOTION SCHEDULE EXAMPLE

Promotions	Hours	Promotion	Days To Promote	Hours Completed
Email Signature	1	Coming Soon Link	All Month	15 Minutes
Database	1	Create Welcome Letter	All Month	1 Hour
Website/ Blog	1	Update Layout	Friday	3
Social Media	5	Visit Reader's Groups	M/T/ W/Sa	7
Sites/Blogs	1	Visit Review Sites	Th	3
Newsletter	2	Create New Newsletter	Saturday	3
Blog Tours				
Articles	2	Write 2 Articles	Sunday	1
Groups	2	Visit My Groups	Friday	1
Forums	1	Visit Writing Forums	Sunday	1
Book Clubs	1	Visit Book Clubs	Tuesday	2

Promotions	Hours	Promotion	Days To Promote	Hours Completed
Radio	2	2 Radio Interviews	Mondays	2
Magazines	1	2 Magazine Interviews	Friday	1
Podcasts	3	Create 2 Podcasts	Saturday	4
Events				

ONLINE PROMOTION PLAN
PROMOTION SCHEDULE

Promotions	Hours	Promotion	Days To Promote	Hours Completed
Email Signature				
Database				
Website/ Blog				
Social Media				
Sites/Blogs				
Newsletter				
Blog Tours				
Articles				
Groups				
Forums				
Book Clubs				
Radio				
Magazines				

Promotions	Hours	Promotion	Days To Promote	Hours Completed
Podcasts				
Events				

CONFERENCE/LITERARY EVENTS TO ATTEND

Event Name	Date	Did You Attend

CONTENT FOR BLOG WORKSHEET

Date	Content

ARTICLES WORKSHEET

Article Title	Submitted To	Date Submitted	Date Published

CONTENT FOR NEWSLETTER WORKSHEET

Content	Date

SOCIAL MEDIA SITES WORKSHEET

Social Media Sites	Date Joined

SITES/BLOGS TO VISIT WORKSHEET

Sites/Blogs	Date Visited

BLOG TOUR SITES WORKSHEET

Sites	Request Letter Sent	Date Scheduled	Date Published

FORUMS/GROUPS/LISTS INTRO WORKSHET

Forums/Groups/Lists	Intro Letter Sent	Date	Date Published

ONLINE BOOK CLUB WORKSHEET

Online Book Club	Intro Letter Sent	Discussion Date	Thank You Sent

ONLINE RADIO WORKSHEET

Online Radio	Intro Letter Sent	Interview Date	Thank You Sent

ONLINE MAGAZINE WORKSHEET

Online Magazine	Intro Letter Sent	Interview Date	Thank You Sent

ONLINE CHATS WORKSHEET

Online Chat/With	Date	Thank You Letter

ONLINE EVENTS WORKSHEET

Online Events	Intro Letter Sent	Discussion Date	Thank You Sent

PODCASTS WORKSHEET

Podcasts	Intro Letter Sent	Interview Date	Thank You Sent

VIDEOS WORKSHEET

Videos	Intro Letter Sent	Interview Date	Thank You Sent

CONFERENCE/LITERARY EVENTS WORKSHEET

Conference/Literary Event With	Date	Thank You Letter

Need Help?

You can never put everything you know into one book, however if you find you need more help with your promotion, I would like to tell you about the program I created to help writers and businesses with their online promotion.

Virtual Tea With LaShaunda is a coaching program that works hand-in-hand with this book. You get the chance to work with me and receive more advance training in the different lessons or you can create your own plan.

I offer one-on-one or group training. If you would like to learn more about *Virtual Tea With LaShaunda*, contact me at lchwriter@gmail.com.

My goal is to help you reach more readers. Together we can create a plan that will help you get in front of the readers looking for your books.

See ya on the net,

LaShaunda C. Hoffman
lashaundahoffman.com
lchwriter@gmail.com

Made in the USA
Columbia, SC
03 February 2018